COUNTRY IS KING!

GARTH BROOKS

Originally hired as a songwriter, he auditioned in a record producer's Nashville office... and was signed up on the spot.

GEORGE STRAIT

Disillusioned and dismayed, he was ready to give up his career and build cattle pens for a living. Then his big break came... and he never looked back.

BILLY RAY CYRUS

He once had hopes of becoming a Major League pitcher, but he gave his "Achy Breaky Heart" to country ... and released the fastest selling debut album in country music history.

VINCE GILL

He's an Oklahoma country boy with a love for bluegrass music who dreamed of making it big... as a professional golfer.

PLUS:
**CLINT BLACK ... RANDY TRAVIS ...
ALAN JACKSON. ..TRAVIS TRITT...
RICKY VAN SHELTON**

HOT COUNTRY

MIKE KOSSER

AVON BOOKS ▲ NEW YORK

HOT COUNTRY is an original publication of Avon Books. This work has never before appeared in book form.

AVON BOOKS
A division of
The Hearst Corporation
1350 Avenue of the Americas
New York, New York 10019

Copyright © 1993 by Mike Kosser
Cover and interior photographs copyright © 1988, 1989, 1990, 1991, 1992 by Alan L. Mayor
Published by arrangement with the author
Library of Congress Catalog Card Number: 92-93918
ISBN: 0-380-77061-X

First Avon Books Printing: April 1993

AVON TRADEMARK REG. U.S. PAT. OFF. AND IN OTHER COUNTRIES, MARCA REGISTRADA, HECHO EN U.S.A.

Printed in the U.S.A.

RA   10   9   8   7   6   5   4   3   2   1

In addition to all the country hunks whose musical lives are the subject of this book, I would like to thank Rick Blackburn, Al Cooley, Nick Hunter, Kim Williams, Doug Grau, Jim Della Croce, Buzz Ledford, Carl Jackson, Mark Wright, David Ross, Frank Dycus, Ed Morris, Doug Baker, Woody Bomar, Jim McBride, Martha Sharp, Ronnie Pugh, and Jim Foglesong for their time and knowledge. Their names are listed in the order in which their interview tapes came tumbling out of my cabinet.

I would also like to thank Maggie Cavender, Jerry Thompson, Bobby Braddock, and the Armstrongs: Beverly, Gerry and Tom C., without whom this book would have been impossible, and Alan Mayor, whose photographs are fabulous.

Also my wife and friend Gina, without whom this book would have been unnecessary, my editor, David Highfill, and my agent, Bob Robison, without whom this book would have been irrelevant.

Most of all, I'd like to thank the country music fans. The truth is, they, and no one else, are the ones who anoint the stars of country music.

Contents

1

A National Passion

OVER THE PAST TWO YEARS COUNTRY MUSIC HAS exploded into a national passion far beyond the expectations of anybody inside or outside the music business.

Consequently, our magazines, newspapers, TV, and radio have pursued the most successful artists and told and retold their various stories, or at least parts of their stories.

But it takes a lot of smart, dedicated people to make a star. These people have stories to tell, and when you put them all together you get a wide panorama of the country music explosion—the stuff they don't tell you about in the magazines and on TV.

Turning the pages of this book, you'll notice familiar names and their stories, some of which you already know. But you'll also see a new perspective, one that feels less like publicist's hype and much more like the real thing. That's because the people telling these stories all have vast experience and understanding of the music they deal with every day of their lives.

A few years back Ricky Van Shelton burst onto the

country scene, his gorgeous smile just about halfway between the brim of his straw Resistol cowboy hat and the neckline of his white undershirt. The hat, the smile, and the undershirt appeared in videos and in numerous publicity photographs. The wise old heads of the CBS Records marketing department had finally gone public with the nasty little secret known to country stars for nearly half a century: country girls *love* country hunks! And they loved Ricky Van Shelton— a million albums at a time. All it took was hit songs and a great singing country hunk.

The first country hunk may have been Ernest Tubb. One of country's early honky-tonk singers, Ernest had a look that would today be called "interesting" rather than gorgeous, glamorous, or magnificent, but the truth is that millions of country girls would have gladly waltzed across Texas with the Texas Troubadour.

A letter to the editor of a fan magazine back in 1945 will give you an idea of what Ernest Tubb meant to female country fans a half century ago: " . . . You really don't know how to appreciate Ernest's singing until you see him when he sings. 'You Nearly Lose Your Mind.' That low note he does on 'trifle' just simply sends me. . . . Ernest is truly my Frank Sinatra."

You might say that Ernest Tubb was the opening act for the most magnificent of all the early country hunks—the incomparable Hank Williams.

Hank had a way of hunching over the microphone and moaning out his country blues that made the young females (and quite a few of the older ones too) feel special. Like Ernest Tubb, Hank Williams was a combination of earthy masculinity and gentle vulnerability that many women find irresistible. When Hank died, women across America mourned, and it seemed that half of them were present at his funeral. After Hank came Elvis, and Elvis filled today's definition of "hunk" to the letter. Filled it? He defined it! As masculine as he looked, and acted, he had a pretty face, in the Hollywood tradition. The snarl in the corner of his upper lip was just the right touch to put his prettiness in its place.

But as country as Elvis was, his image was not, and neither was most of his music. And when Elvis's tremendous pop appeal allowed him to dominate the country charts, a number of country music executives appealed to the trade magazines to get Elvis *off* their country charts. They did, and he stayed off the top of the country charts for many years.

In the meantime, country music almost died.

By 1961 there were only eighty-one radio stations across America playing country music full time. The coming of Elvis and the going of Hank had apparently combined to drive many young women away from country music and women are, and have always been, the backbone of country music's popularity.

Or had they really gone away? The Country Music Association, which is a commercial organization, not a music appreciation society, did not think so. Slowly, painstakingly, they started promoting country music to struggling radio stations that were searching for a money-making format. Within a few years, the eighty-one stations were upwards of six hundred and growing like a hound puppy every year (on the way to a current total of more than twenty-five hundred radio stations across the country).

By 1975 country music was making joyful noises nationwide and many of the most joyful were being made by men like Merle Haggard, Charley Pride, Johnny Cash, Buck Owens, Waylon Jennings, Conway Twitty, Charlie Rich, Billy "Crash" Craddock, Cal Smith, George Jones, and a dozen other true radio heroes. But where were the hunks? By Presley standards, true hunks were guys who had thousands of young girls mobbing their concerts, screaming and crying, longing and dreaming, and most of the young girls were long gone from country music.

Then came the outlaw movement, modern country's first major on-purpose bid for acceptance in the pop, or "crossover," music world. Willie and Waylon and Kris sold a lot of records, and there is no doubt that Kristofferson achieved the status of hunkdom, primarily through his movies, but there was still something missing. In the big cities, too many fans of the outlaws seemed to consider them a hippie's answer to the reactionary world of country music or (as the Urban Cowboy phase kicked in) a sort of campy, snide, elitist masquerade where everybody dresses up in cowboy suits and rhinestones, and shouts "ya-*hoo*" and drinks long-neck Lone Star, and at least talks about riding the mechanical bull, an experience to be quickly forgotten as soon as the next fad comes along.

At that time, too many country records were being made with at least one eye on the so-called crossover market, to fill the needs of major market radio stations. This did not necessarily have much to do with the needs of the folks who bought country records. The results often sounded watered down, middle-of-the-road, certainly lacking in the kind of energy and attitude that made traditional country so much more fun to listen to, dance to, and sing along with.

And then in 1984 came the second near-death of country music. This one was more a media event than the first, based on a *New York Times* article by Robert Palmer. The piece had a ring of truth to it, for it noted the coming of a new group of young country artists with more traditional sounds than the eclectic heroes of the seventies. But there is something in the national media that seems to despise southern (or rural) culture in general and country music in particular, and so the various newspeople who picked up the story tended to dwell on the death—in fact, it seemed that they were much more interested in the death of country music than they had ever been in its life.

The following year a young man from North Carolina named Randy Travis hit the country charts for the first time with a song called "On the Other Hand." He was definitely from the Lefty Frizzell/ Merle Haggard school of country singing but it seemed he took the style one step further. Recorded dry, with a minimum of blurring echo, his voice slid precisely from note to note. And everything about Travis, from his song delivery to his manner of speaking to the very look on his face, was so uncompromisingly country and sincere that a year later, when his singles all turned into hits and his albums began to fly off the shelves into the anxious hands of young record buyers, every major record label in Nashville began to turn America's honky-tonks inside out in search of singers as country as Travis.

Not that Randy was the first of his era to bring country back to its honky-tonk roots. George Strait had been having hits for several years, but without the monster record sales. Nashville record executives tended to think of him as sort of a cowboy freak. Ricky Skaggs was also finding sales and critical success with his bluegrass-based style, and Hank Williams, Jr., was probably selling most of all, though his music may have been closer to the southern rockers than to the heart of country.

''So find me another Travis'' echoed down the corridors of Music Row.

They searched, and they found. One after another: Ricky Van Shelton, Clint Black, Garth Brooks, Alan Jackson, Doug Stone, Travis Tritt, Joe Diffie, Mark Chesnutt, Collin Raye, Tracy Lawrence. There seemed to be no end to them. And they were so unlike their predecessors of the past twenty years. Instead of trying to water down their country so they could ''cross over'' onto the pop charts (an effort that rarely succeeded), these new stars sang as country as they chose in front of steel guitars and fiddles, not Mantovani strings, with tight two and three part harmonies, not the vanilla effects of studio backup vocal groups.

Oh, and they wore hats. My, did they wear hats. (Except for, notably, the guy who inspired the movement, the redoubtable Mr. Travis.) And why not? Hats, cowboy hats, are an honorable country tradition. Ernest Tubb wore one. Hank Williams wore one. Bluegrass star Lester Flatt wore one and the father of bluegrass, Bill Monroe, still wears one. These new country stars saw their hats as a way to relate to the traditional old country stars.

So many of the new stars wear hats that a few years back, unkind agent and manager types began to refer to them as "hat acts," and arguments began to arise concerning whether or not artists like Randy Travis and Doug Stone were really "hat acts," even though they didn't wear hats. In other words, had "hat acts" become a generic term more descriptive of a type of music than a style of haberdashery?

By 1991 it had become clear that one country act was beginning to tower over all the rest. He was an Oklahoman named Garth Brooks, and of all the exciting newcomers he least fit the definition of hunk. Van Shelton was a hunk. All you had to do was look at him and you knew! Alan Jackson was a hunk, one picture was certainly worth *that* word. Randy Travis fit the definition, and so did George Strait. As for Clint Black, no telling how many girls haven't recovered since the first time they spotted him in a video on CMT.

But Garth was different. While most of these new hotshots were built to model Wrangler jeans, Garth was into wearing shirts with broad, vertical stripes to disguise his baby-fat paunch. And he wasn't fooling himself, either. "It's funny how a chubby kid can just be having fun, and they call that entertaining," he told a nationwide audience the night he was named Country Music Association entertainer of the year.

And it works for Garth. He's no late-era Elvis, struggling to preserve a fading image of glamour. Like an ideal marriage, Garth's fans know him, warts and all, and they love him just the way he is. How much do they love him? To the tune of twenty million albums sold in twenty-one months. At the beginning of 1992, Garth's first three albums occupied the top three slots on *Billboard* magazine's country album charts. On the pop charts, Garth's albums were numbers one, three, and thirteen. If the fifties belonged to Elvis, the sixties to the Beatles, the seventies to the BeeGees and the eighties to Michael Jackson, surely the decade of the nineties has begun in possession of the chubby kid from Oklahoma.

Ask most people in the music business why Garth is so incredibly successful and they will only shake their heads in wonder, but that is no putdown of Garth. The fact is, any act that successful defies explanation. Nevertheless, there are opinions. For example, Edward Morris, country editor of *Billboard*, says, "He has a peculiar sense of sensitivity and roughness as exemplified in 'The Dance.' . . . I mean, here he does a video that encapsulates John Wayne, Keith Whitley, a rodeo rider who was gored to death by a bull, Martin Luther King, and he stands in front of a gray backdrop and introduces this thing and . . . of course [the song] is pop philosophy . . . but I don't think it works against him . . . it becomes almost everybody's anthem for risk-taking and it's done with such gentleness and sensitivity. . . ." Sound familiar? A restatement of the qualities that made Ernest Tubb and Hank Williams so popular in their day? Strip Garth down to his essentials and he becomes that magical mythical country paragon, the man of power who's not afraid to show his feelings.

But before Garth there was Randy Travis. He came along at a time when country music was just begin-

ning to creep out of its lounge lizard stage. Record
sales were way down and so were the ratings of many
radio stations, and yet those stations continued to play
all the old country artists, whose careers were obviously winding down. In other words, too many of the
major country stations still thought of country music
as the adult alternative to the old middle-of-the-road
elevator music. For awhile it became almost impossible to break a brand new act. In Nashville record
executives were beginning to get nervous. Jobs were
on the line. Aspirin and other more potent painkillers
were rampant.

And then came Travis, selling so many albums
that the label executives stood up on their hind
legs, started signing new artists and demanding airplay from radio. Suddenly all sorts of new stars
were exploding onto the country horizon. Some of
them, like Baillie and the Boys and Foster and
Lloyd, racked up a lot more airplay than they did
sales while others, like the Kentucky Headhunters
and Dwight Yoakam, found their sales soaring far
out of proportion to their airplay. There were some
female artists beginning to shine: Kathy Mattea,
Lorrie Morgan, Patty Loveless, K. T. Oslin, and a
resurgent Tanya Tucker, to name but a few. But
country has been a world of men singing for the
womenfolk since long before the country charts
consisted of "29 guys and Kitty Wells," and it's
the guys who are really changing the way the
whole world looks at country music.

But why? What is the big difference between now
and 1984? Again, Ed Morris: "I can't think it entirely
accidental that it megaboomed in the mid-eighties

right after TNN [The Nashville Network] started getting some currency as well as CMT [Country Music
Television]...

"... Country music was always presented to the
world rather episodically... occasionally you would
see somebody on television and occasionally someone
would break through in the fan magazines... Before
TNN and CMT you had to go out and get country
music, you had to tune in your station and keep it
there. You had to read your newspapers and go to
country concerts but all of a sudden now on a daily
drumbeat basis it was coming into your home... and
I think that had something to do with showing that
country was more complex and prettier, or profound
than the stereotype I mean, before that, what did you
have? 'Hee Haw'!"

Ed Morris touches on the truth subtly rather than
landing on it with both feet. The drumbeat he was
talking about beats largely for the country hunks,
those photogenic phenoms who are selling most of the
records. During Randy Travis's early days on Warner
Brothers Records, he was constantly appearing as a
guest on Ralph Emery's "Nashville Now" cable TV
show. And if you wonder how a little cable talk show
can help a country singer sell millions of records, reflect on the fact that Mr. Emery's *Memories* appeared
on the *New York Times Book Review* best-sellers' list
for many weeks.

David Ross, editor and publisher of *Music Row*,
Nashville's most respected homegrown music publication, had this to say about country's expanded appeal:

"In the eighties, what was on [every country star's]

bio, what was the real in vogue thing for all the artists, was that they grew up listening to the Opry on the front porch with their father and their grandfather, and they had an outhouse, and if they were switching over from another format [such as pop] then that didn't matter because in their heart they were always country. Now, it's changed a little bit. I think we're seeing a reaction to the pop marketplace that has gotten out of touch with the real world. I mean, rap music, even the pop stars like a Madonna, have kind of spiraled up on ego stairways and a few of them. . . have been able to pull it off successfully, but there's a lot of them posturing and taking attitudes, and I think a lot of the fans, the consumers, are just fed up with it all. They're just thinking to themselves 'I don't relate to this, what do I need this for?'

"So I think country has really hit a nerve because country musicians have always had a sort of humble attitude. It stems from the bluegrass days, it stems from the very heavy religious overtones that the bluegrass music came from. . . a lot of these country musicians are from very religious areas of the country as well and humility and a humble attitude is almost a way of life. It's kind of a personality trait which is perceived as a very positive way to be."

Just as President Bush struck a welcome chord when he talked about a kinder, gentler nation, the public likes these kinder, gentler hunks. Perhaps part of it is the economy. Although the administration sensed a recession in 1991, many Americans have been losing economic ground throughout the eighties and when times are hard, people like to believe that even if they are not a howling "success," they can be respected for what they've got in their hearts. Such people may suspect that a Madonna or a Rod Stewart would not respect a poor but honest, hardworking yeoman, but that Randy Travis or Garth Brooks would.

Nine years after its media funeral, country music is riding higher than anybody ever dreamed. At this writing, approximately twenty percent of the entries on the pop album charts are country. Besides Brooks, Clint Black, Alan Jackson, George Strait, Travis Tritt, Vince Gill, and Randy Travis, there is a wave of newcomer hunks like Collin Raye, Tracy Lawrence, Mark Collie, Sammy Kershaw, and Hal Ketchum.

A new force in country music is group hunk, the proposition that female country fans are bound to find some hunks among the many male country groups that are beginning to riddle the charts with hits. You might remember that until Alabama came along in 1981, country fans resisted falling in love with groups. Perhaps they associated groups with dope-smoking hippie pop stars. Whatever the reason, they rejected bands like the Eagles, Poco, Pure Prairie League, and the Flying Burrito Brothers no matter how country they sounded, and often they sounded a *lot* more country than some of the so-called country stars that had permeated radio by the end of the seventies.

The eighties saw country attitudes toward groups soften somewhat. Southern Pacific, Desert Rose Band, the Oak Ridge Boys, SKB, the Nitty Gritty Dirt Band, the O'Kanes, the Gatlin Brothers and others all had an impact; but only Alabama and the Oaks had the kind of record sales that showed strong fan loyalty.

All that is changing. Restless Heart, Diamond Rio, and Confederate Railroad have all shown sales power, and more groups are on the way.

One particularly exciting group is the Remingtons, who hit the top ten with their first single and haven't stopped running since. Another exciting new group is Little Texas, described by veteran music publisher Woody Bomar as follows: "I've seen the women react to them in television performances. I've seen how they [Warner Brothers] present them in videos . . . as the young, sex symbol group!" But the most successful of all up and coming groups might be the powerful Arista duo of Brooks and Dunn.

Most of the music business people I talked to are naturally very excited by country music's huge surge over the past several years. Words of caution, however, were sounded by two very well respected members of the Nashville music community. Nick Hunter of Giant Records, one of the most outspoken figures in the world of country music record promotion, agreed that country music is a more powerful force in the record business today than it had been, but insisted the difference is not as great as everybody thinks.

"The impression that country is as hot as it is," he points out, "goes back to one thing, and that's SoundScan." Nick is referring to the electronic record sales tally system that *Billboard* magazine started using just a couple of years ago to give a quick and accurate count of whose records are selling where. "And I will give you an example of what I mean," he continues. "We had the Randy Travis album, *Always and Forever*, which is over four million [units sold], approaching five. . . . The album chart systems (both country and pop) would call the accounts [the stores]; the accounts. . . would give them. . . their best sellers. Most people. . . did not give. . . a piece count [but] gave them what they *thought* were their best sellers, which opened a lot of chart positions [to deals like] 'Hey, I'll send you ten freebies for a report'—that was not an unusual process back in those days.''

Nick is saying that because the stores did not have to offer proof of sales to justify telling the trade magazines that this or that album was among their best sellers, the record label marketing people were not above bribing store managers with free product to sell in order to get favorable sales reports that would help their artists on the album charts.

''But when *Always And Forever* was the biggest selling country album, which it was for I don't know how many weeks . . . we would call them [record stores] and ask them what their number one country album was and they would say, 'Oh, Randy's always up there. In fact, it's the biggest selling album we have in the store.'

'' 'Well, what did you report it [for the] pop [chart]?'

'' 'Well I didn't,' [they would answer]. 'It wasn't a pop album.'

''And, it could have even been outselling the album they reported number one pop two to one.'' It might be appropriate to add here that the pop album charts are supposed to rate the hottest selling albums, regardless of the genre. In fact, as you'll see again and again later on, the *Billboard* pop album charts no longer even use the term pop, in order to emphasize their universal inclusiveness.

"What SoundScan has done," Nick adds, "is to put everyone on equal footing. And my view of country in a strange way is, yes we're hot, but we're not as hot as people think we are [because] we weren't as cold as a lot of people thought we were... before, a country album very seldom ever reached the pop charts, or when it did it reached the lower echelons because of this manual reporting system. But now when it is all SoundScan, everybody's on the same equal basis, so therefore... Garth and Hammer, and Travis Tritt and Madonna and all those people are pretty much all on the same plane. It's whoever's actually selling the records."

In other words, the huge sales of Randy Travis a few years back did not make as big a splash among the media and the record industry as Garth's monster albums of today because the pop album charts of the time did not accurately reflect the popularity of country music. These positive or negative perceptions in the media of country music's popularity are very important to the country music industry.

What will it take to maintain country music's extraordinary momentum?

The answer might lie in the next country hunk. While it's difficult to imagine another Garth Brooks, just as it would have been difficult to imagine another Elvis Presley back in the early rock 'n roll years, his successor might already be with us, among the seven or eight hot country hunks, or the dozens of contenders who are already elbowing their way into the furious competition for the hearts and wallets of country fans, or among the brand new ones who are just beginning to be heard. As this book goes to press, Billy Ray Cyrus is still selling albums like no other first album in history. More on Billy Ray later.

Hot Country will take you into the world of the young men who are transforming pop music, perhaps even bringing together the generations as has not been done since the rock 'n roll revolution split them apart. You'll learn what it is that makes them tick. You'll hear it from them, from the people who work with them, and from the people who watch their videos and buy their records. If you are already a country fan, Hot Country will bring you closer to the guys you love to see and hear. If you're not a country fan but are curious, this book will make you turn on the radio and tune in the stations you've been avoiding.

2

New Hunks

AS I MENTIONED EARLIER IN THIS BOOK, BACK IN 1984 the media announced the death of country music. Never mind that there were still more than two thousand radio stations all over America playing nothing but country music; country sales were down and country music was short on new heroes, so the media decided that the body was cold and stiff. Now, nearly a decade later, you can tell how hot country is: TV and print have it by the throat and are shaking it until they've squeezed every dollar out of it. You can't open *People* magazine or *Time* without catching sight of a Stetson hat or two. Even the *Enquirer* has sunk its jaws into Garth Brooks.

Many of the people involved in this media explosion don't know a hell of a lot about country music. Yesterday they were covering the Oscars and the day before they were working on something else. They probably don't even care if they get it right. It's *only* country music, and, anyway, they've got a very short deadline. Recently a friend of mine who is a veteran of many years in country TV journalism contacted a Hollywood group that was producing a TV sitcom about country music in Nashville. He suggested that they might be able to use the talents of someone who knew what country music in Nashville is really like.

Their reply: "*We* don't need somebody in Nashville to tell *us* how to do a show on country music." Well, their show may or may not be a hit, but as they say down on the bayou, gua-rawn-*tee* that they'll get it all wrong, just as they've been getting it all wrong ever since they cast George Hamilton as Hank Williams in *Your Cheatin' Heart*.

A lot of myths grow up in the entertainment business because infotainment journalists are more into the "tainment" than the "info" part of their job. One of them was recently pointed out to me by a songwriter friend who has in his lifetime written some major hits.

"All I read about," he said, "is that all these new hit artists are such great hit songwriters, but I just took a look on the country hot singles charts, and here's what I found: out of seventy-five songs on this week's chart, only fourteen of them were written by the artists singing them, and out of those fourteen, nine of them were cowritten with a 'real' songwriter."

Interesting, but more a plus for the industry than a minus. What it means is that, as much as these writer/ artists would like to see their own songs dancing at the top of the charts, most of them are smart enough to know that a successful recording career today demands the very best songs an artist can find, whether he or somebody else writes them.

How does a country artist find hit songs? There are dozens of music publishing companies in Nashville and elsewhere whose job is to find great songs and pitch them to appropriate artists. The artists usually rely on their record producers (the individuals who direct their recording sessions) and A & R people (the people at record labels who discover and sign artists) to find songs for them.

The A & R people and producers listen to hundreds of songs, narrow them down to dozens, then meet with the artists to decide which songs will be recorded for the next album. It's a difficult process, involving many changes of mind that drives publishers and songwriters crazy. Yes, we're recording your song. No, we didn't record your song. Yes, your song will be the next single. No, we changed our minds.

For artists who write much of their own material, it's sometimes difficult for them to hear the quality of another songwriter's music given the personal feelings that went into their own songs. Their producers and A & R people must sometimes work hard to convince them. The artists who continue to record the best songs available to them have a much better chance of staying on top than those who let their egos interfere.

Now that you know more than you ever thought you wanted to know about songs, singers, and entertainment journalists, let's talk about some of the young artists who have been doing such great recording over the past year or two. At this time, there have been eight or nine whose names are ablaze in the country world, but there are a surprising number who are just a notch below. These up-and-comers are already selling better than yesterday's country superstars sold during most of their careers. Most of them

Producer James Stroud (left) presents Tracy Lawrence with a Harley for his first gold album.

are handsome and sing well and were totally unheard of three years ago. There are also a couple of them who have been around for awhile and are beginning to rise to new heights.

One of the hunkier looking ones is also one of the youngest, and one of the hottest. He's Tracy Lawrence, the son of an Arkansas banker, and at the time this is being written his first album on Atlantic Records, *Sticks And Stones*, is riding the pop album charts. Just a few years ago that would have meant that he was cutting pop sounding records for country radio stations. But today is different from a few years ago. Tracy Lawrence is just as country sounding as his cowboy hat would make you think. He shines on videos, with his fair hair, clipped mustache, and dimples. His album has already reached gold status (five hundred thousand copies sold), and is still bringing in heavy sales reports. Just a few years back such a hot debut album would have had the country record industry hyperventilating, but in this day of hot country hunks, the industry is merely excited about Tracy Lawrence.

There are some who complain that they have trouble identifying new country acts by their voices because so many radio stations refuse to allow their disc jockeys (they call them air personalities these days) to identify the records or the artists. Critics who attempt to describe the singing of these new artists underscore the alleged problem. A *Miami Herald* reviewer, for example, described Tracy Lawrence's vocal style as "a little bit of Garth Brooks, a dash of George Jones and just a smidgen of Keith Whitley," while a *New York Newsday* reporter calls him a "direct descendant of Lefty Frizzell, Merle Haggard and his hero, George Strait." A number of other hot young country acts would easily fit these descriptions, but I think that as we get used to hearing them, and as some of them continue to mature and develop, we won't have much trouble telling them apart. Remember that when Conway Twitty first came out with "It's Only Make Believe," many people thought he was Elvis, but today any veteran country fan knows Conway when he hears him.

Tracy Lawrence was just a couple of months short of stardom when a trio of thugs almost ended his life in a Nashville parking lot. The three men, two of them armed, robbed Tracy and a lady friend and then decided they wanted to take them up to the girl's room. Assuming that the three men intended to assault her and then kill them both, Tracy tried to wrestle the gun away from one of them. The girl escaped, but Tracy wound up with four bullet wounds, facing a three month convalescence that turned into six weeks. Stardom was waiting for the twenty-three-year-old and he must have been in a hurry to catch it.

There are *some* similarities between Tracy Lawrence and John Anderson. The long golden curly locks, for example. And the Lefty Frizzell vocal heritage. And a hard country album stepping smartly around the pop album charts. But that's where the similarity ends. Tracy's fans think he's cute. John isn't. He looks more like Buffalo Bill—or maybe a buffalo. And Tracy got started yesterday, while John, it seems, got started yesteryear. Remember "Swingin' "? That was in 1983 and it sold 1.3 million copies back in those legendary days when singles still counted in country music. John had a bunch of other classic hits that first time around, including "I'm Just An Old Chunk Of Coal," "Wild And Blue," and "I Just Came Home To Count The Memories," to name a few. If you remember those hits, you'll understand that the way John Anderson sings, he ought to feel more at home now than he did in the John Travolta era of country music.

After 1986, Anderson's recording career came to a grinding halt. Nashville didn't forget how good he was. Two labels signed him and failed to cut hits on him. He thought he was still making good records. Imagine what it must have felt like to be a former

John Anderson

hitmaker who still sang great, and yet every record you put out just died quietly.

Then BNA Records signed him. Or rather a brand new label, a subsidiary of RCA, signed him. He'd have an album out just as soon as they were organized and ready to go, they told him. But a new record label is *never* ready to go as soon as anyone thinks it will be. This new label didn't even have a name yet. And when they decided to call themselves BNA Entertainment, what in the world did the BNA stand for anyhow?

Obviously they *were* ready when, at long last, John got his album release. The name of the album was *Seminole Wind* and not long after its release it hit the country charts. Just a short time later it was top ten country, and also top one hundred on that ''*Billboard* 200 Top

Albums'' chart that we call the pop album chart. The cause of all this excitement was the first single off the album, ''Straight Tequila Night,'' John's first number one smash since the Paleozoic Era.

As an artist, John Anderson is impossible to figure. He sings so country that his popularity in the early 1980s might have cued folks that a new traditional country revival was coming. But, as Nashville journalist Thomas Goldsmith once wrote, ''He was as likely to cover the Rolling Stones as Lefty Frizzell and scored hits with tunes by both acts.''

John Anderson has barely begun his career revival, so it's a little early to judge just how far he can go. But he is a singer and songwriter of great talent and originality. Combine these elements with his years of experience and the thirty-eight-year-old from Apopka, Florida, seems likely to settle down to a long and prosperous phase two.

What does it take for a singer to get record executives excited enough to want to make him a star? It used to be that a tape demo with a good voice was enough, but these days, with videos such an important promotional tool, they like to see what a singer looks like onstage. Especially, they like to see what he can do to a crowd.

In Nashville there are several clubs, most notably Douglas Corner and Bluebird Cafe, where singers stage showcases for themselves. One of these hopefuls is a young man from Doniphan, Missouri, named Billy Yates. Billy cuts hair at the Hair Pavilion, a popular beauty establishment on Nashville's Music Row. As he stands over his customers, scissors and comb in hand, he can look out from his huge second story window at the music business passing him by on the street. Across the street is WSIX-FM, one of the country's more important country radio stations. Fifty yards down the street to his right is Sony-Tree, Nashville's most potent music publishing company. Within two blocks of where he stands, snipping and clipping, songs are being written and recorded, and stars are being made. Half the time Billy must feel like the poor kid with his nose pressed against the window pane of a candy store.

Does Billy Yates feel that the world, or at least country music, is passing him by? He smiles a good-natured grin and takes another snip off the top of a shaggy studio musician.

"Maybe a few months ago I might have felt that way," he says. "It goes up and down, you know. Sometimes you feel like you've got something going, and sometimes it feels like the pits. But lately, it's been pretty good."

Over the past year Billy has done a number of showcases at Douglas Corner. An accomplished graphic artist, he designs his own invitations with western motifs and sends them out to record company executives and employees. Some of them come, and some of them don't. What they see is a good show, backed by some of Nashville's best studio musicians, friends of Billy's who play without charge, and receive haircuts in exchange. He's an excellent country singer in the new traditional mode, and he knows the way to a bar crowd's heart. His showcases are generally stompin' successes.

"The last six months I've had a lot of interest from the labels," he says. "People asking me to send them demo tapes, and then Horipro [a new Nashville publishing company founded by Nashville publishing legend Bob Beckham] signed me to a writing deal. We cut some real good sessions and I think we're getting close to a record deal with one of the major labels.''

Billy has also received many requests to sing on demos—recordings made by publishers and writers to show off their songs for singers. He is glad to do it for the money, for the studio experience, and because it helps to make people on Music Row familiar with the sound of Billy Yates.

Will Billy Yates have a record out by the time this book is published? That's his hope, but Billy has been roughing it on the streets of Nashville for five years now and he knows that most good things take a long time to happen, if they happen at all. But if it does happen for Billy, one of the main ingredients might be those live showcases at Douglas Corner. It just so happens that about a month after my conversation with Billy, he called to say that Curb Records wanted to sign him to a deal. Not long after that call, the contract had been written, and various lawyers had been appointed to bless the contract. The signings came not long after. Needless to say, Billy Yates was in a golden daze, but five years of being knocked around Nashville like a hockey puck can make a man cautious.

If talent means anything, by the time this book is in the bookstores, many of you will have heard the music of Billy Yates. A major recording career is about to begin.

You might say that Mark Chesnutt's major recording career began on the stage at Cutter's nightclub in

Beaumont, Texas. That's where producer Mark Wright, who earlier had launched Clint Black's recording career, first watched Chesnutt perform.

Chesnutt was then in his mid-twenties but already a veteran of nearly a decade in the honky-tonks, including a stint at Gilley's when he was only seventeen. During this time he had begun to take trips to Nashville in search of songs and a record deal. He found a great song, "Too Cold At Home," and recorded it on the Houston-based Cherry label. Today it's almost impossible for an independent record label to promote a hit. Fortunately for Mark Chesnutt, his drummer, Roger Montgomery, is a former member of George Strait's band and had some music business savvy. He got MCA Records' regional promotion man, Roger Ramsey Corkill, to hear the record, and Corkill was so impressed that he delivered the record personally to Tony Brown, Vice President for A & R at MCA Records, and one of Nashville's most influential music figures. "His voice was too good to be true and the song was a hit," Brown recalls. "So I flew down to see him, and that's all she wrote."

Tony Brown brought Mark Wright in on the project, and Wright decided to catch Mark Chesnutt's live act on his home turf. An artist can't have a better showcase than that. Chesnutt was *the star* at Cutter's, drawing mobs of wildly enthusiastic patrons to see him in the middle of the week.

All it took was one show and Wright was just as enthusiastic about Chesnutt as the fans. They became fast friends and soon they were in the studio cutting hits, including the now-classic "Too Cold At Home." The single was a smash and the album went gold. Pro

Mark Chesnutt

that he is, Mark Chesnutt is quick to give credit to the song:

"That's my favorite song in the world. . . . I was going to Nashville quite a bit trying to find a deal, and I said, 'Man, if I never record another song again in my life, I want to do that.' I had a feeling about that song."

Other Mark Chesnutt hits include "Broken Promise Land" and "Old Flames Have New Names," the smash hit written by Bobby Braddock and Rafe Van Hoy.

All real country fans know that one of Garth

Brooks's signature songs is "Friends in Low Places," but only Mark Chesnutt fans and a few fanatics know that Mark had the song on an album before Garth's single came out. No matter, Mark has had plenty of hits on his own, and plenty of hits to come.

Many of the new traditional country hitmakers follow the Lefty Frizzell/Merle Haggard vocal tradition. Sammy Kershaw's styling is much closer to that of George Jones, but, contrary to the opinion of some critics, he's no Jones clone by any means. His debut Polygram album, *Don't Go Near The Water*, made a deep impression on both the country and pop album charts, thanks to Kershaw's vocals, some sharp production by Buddy Cannon and Norro Wilson, and some excellent songs. The chart-topping single, "Cadillac Style," included in the album, earned Kershaw a job as spokesman for Cadillac's 1992 fall sales campaign in the southwest region. By fall of 1992, the album had gone gold.

Like Mark Chesnutt, Cajun Kershaw started performing in the clubs at a very early age, twelve, and now, twenty-two years and three marriages later, he has had all the experience necessary for success, and then some. "I'm a ballad-singing fool," he says, "and I've lived all those songs at one time or another. There's almost no place I'm more at home than in front of a crowd. I even love it when I have a heckler in the audience, because I can really get something going and have the audience in stitches." Onstage Kershaw is a ball of fire, the kind of entertainer you can tell has a lot of fun in front of an audience.

Kershaw is very knowledgeable about those who

have come before him in country music, a trait shared by many of his hit-making contemporaries. During his early years he performed on shows with many major Nashville stars and he went to school on all of them. Jones is obviously his major hero, but he also claims to have been influenced by Cal Smith and the late Mel Street.

A few years ago he had finally grown weary of the music business and the strain it put on his personal life, so he took a job with the Wal-Mart Corporation, hoping that the steady life-style would be good for his family life. An interesting idea, that. For two years he traveled around the country remodeling Wal-Marts.

He was so good at it and the work was so lucrative that he was in Texas working on starting his own remodeling business when a friend called and suggested he come to Nashville to take a shot at the big time. Like many of country's new stars, he got his record deal with Mercury/Polygram as the result of a live showcase. It's been all open road since then.

Videos play a critical role in the making of new country stars. The small screen brings the fans very close to a singer, sometimes right up his nostrils. And so it's not surprising that so many of these new young stars look great. That's one of the criteria used by labels when they're deciding whether they want to sign a new act. Sammy Kershaw has a great look, and so does Doug Stone. Stone broke into the big time a couple of years ago with one of those records that just grab you and never let go.

"I'd Be Better Off (In a Pine Box)," Doug's very first single on Epic Records, earned him a Grammy nomination. His first album has sold more than half a

Doug Stone performs on "Nashville Now."

million copies and at the time this book is being written is still hanging around both country and pop charts. His follow-up album, *I Thought It Was You*, has also gone gold.

He's about the same age as Kershaw and, yes, he started young. His mom was a singer. She took him with her when she sang and by the time he was seven she had him on the stage. By the time he was fifteen he had graduated to playing skating rinks for five dollars a night. Most kids playing gigs are constantly being reminded by their parents that they ought to be thinking about normal ways of making a living, but to Doug Stone's mother, making a living singing seemed like a perfectly normal thing to do. She continued to encourage him through his struggling years. The family was used to poverty. They lived in a trailer on the side of a mountain with a washing machine set next to the well. Later they moved to Carollton, Georgia, where Doug and his dad set themselves up as mechanics and part-time hog farmers.

Doug became a splendid mechanic. It was a good thing because he wasn't earning much money making music in his little home studio. And then a woman named Phyllis Bennett took a friend's advice to catch Doug's show at the VFW hall in Newnan, Georgia. He must have made an impression on her because a year later she was back, waving a personal management contract at him.

She brought him to the attention of Nashville record producer Doug Johnson and Johnson brought him to then CBS Nashville A & R chief Bob Montgomery. That canny veteran knew a hit talent when he heard one. Doug Stone was now just a hit record away from stardom. The hit (''Pine Box'') came fast.

One more little detail that is now a part of country folklore. Doug Stone was originally Doug Brooks but by the time his national career began there was a Garth Brooks. It just wouldn't do for there to be a pair of country singers on the scene that fans would assume were the Brooks Brothers. Some of his associates came up with the name Stone at just the time he happened to be writing a song titled ''Heart of Stone'' and he couldn't resist the coincidence. Thus

Doug Stone

we now have Doug Stone instead of Doug Brooks or Doug Rivers. When a star gets as big as quickly as Doug Stone has, you somehow get the feeling that the name fits just right.

Every hot hit-making hunk in this book is signed to one of the small circle of worldwide companies known as ''major record labels.'' Every hot hit-making hunk except one, that is. Now is as good a time as any to talk about these labels and how they make the hits.

It used to be that American hits were made by American owned companies, but now it's no longer so. Get this: CBS and MCA are Japanese, Mercury/Polygram is Dutch, Capitol (Liberty in Nashville) is English, and RCA is German. You want to buy American? Buy Warner Brothers. But you'd better hurry. There are no guarantees for the future.

Years ago there were plenty of genuine independent record labels capable of having a hit and building stars. Ovation had the Kendalls. Playboy had Mickey Gilley. Starday had George Jones and Cowboy Copas. But in the eighties, as country radio got more and more competitive, apparently the major record labels and some of their friends at important radio stations squeezed the little guys off the air. In fact, there hasn't been a number one hit on an independent label since a decade ago when Jim Glaser hit the top spot on Noble Vision Records.

But there is one man left in Nashville bold enough and smart enough to fight the big boys and carve out a real place for himself and his label. The man's name is Ray Pennington and his label is called Step One Records. The company is on the third floor of a modest office building a block down from Nashville's Music Row, on Division Street, near all the stores that sell souvenir ash trays to the tourists.

For a small label, Pennington maintains a fairly

large staff, complete with promotion, marketing, publicity, A & R, and administrative personnel. Step One started less than a decade ago and established a positive cash flow with a line of oldie country artists that Pennington was able to telemarket profitably. But Pennington had started in the record business four decades ago in Cincinnati with King Records, the company that brought us Hank Ballard and James Brown, among others. He had also been a successful record producer for RCA Records. Pennington craved the action that comes with having current hit artists.

His first solid shot at hit-making with Step One is a tremendous young talent named Clinton Gregory. A recent single, "Play Ruby Play," was a phenomenal video hit that should have made top ten on the country airplay charts but didn't. Nevertheless, Clinton Gregory is already a country star and his album sales prove it.

We've recounted again and again how young all these country prodigies were when they started. One started at the age of twelve. Another started at seven. Clinton Gregory began playing fiddle at age *three*. Fiddle is a murderous instrument for anybody to do even a fair job on, but this kid was sawing away in his crib. His dad was probably standing over him making sure he got it right, because Clinton represented the fifth generation in a family of fiddlers.

By the time he was four, his dad had given Clinton a brand new fiddle and put him on the show. "Everybody clapped and gave me a few dollars and some change," he recalls. "The next day I was playin' in the backyard; I had some old wood, hammer and nails. My daddy asked me what I was doing and I told him I was building a stage.''

It wasn't until he was sixteen that Clinton moved from Virginia to North Carolina, joined a band, and began to add singing to his fiddle-playing. By 1987 he was playing in Suzy Bogguss's road band. Later he cut a demo recording, paying for the session out of his own pocket. One night, while he was performing in Savannah, Georgia, he played his demo for the steel player who was performing with him. The steel player happened to be Ron Elliott, whose day gig happened to be working as national sales director for Step One Records. Ron was taken by Clinton's rendition of ''Nobody's Darlin' But Mine,'' so he took it with him back to Nashville and played it for the staff at Step One. Step One is like a family. In fact, several of the employees are members of Ray Pennington's family. For the label to sign an act the whole staff has to feel good about the act.

The whole staff *did* feel good about Clinton, and Ray liked the demo of ''Nobody's Darlin' But Mine'' so well that he put *it* out as Clinton's first single, making very few changes. Not long after, Clinton cracked the top twenty of the *R & R* country charts with ''(If It Weren't For Country Music) I'd Go Crazy.'' It was the first time since 1984 that an independent had cracked the top twenty, according to Step One promotion director Buzz Ledford. But what really showed Step One that they had a winner was that the album of the same name began to jump off the shelves into the hands of fans who didn't seem to care that the single wasn't number one or even top ten.

Unlike the major labels, Step One does not have a megamillion dollar sales organization pushing huge numbers of CDs in jewel boxes into the marketplace and hoping that they don't somehow get back more than they send out (there are counterfeiters of CDs that make such things possible). Step One has to fight hard for every market they get. Clinton Gregory makes it easier for them because the folks out there really like him, to the tune of sales of over two hundred thousand on his previous album and fast early sales on his new album, *Freeborn Man*.

I was recently talking to an executive at an important country radio station. He thought Clinton Gregory was "probably the most underrated talent in country music today.

"It'll be interesting," he continued, "to see what happens when his contract with Step One Records is finished. Half the major labels in Nashville will be trying to sign him."

The folks at Step One, of course, are hoping that they'll have the opportunity to reap the full rewards of all the hard work they've put into this exciting and unique country singer and fiddler.

Sometimes career success comes because something happens that has nothing directly to do with what a performer tries to do with his career. Several years ago Bob DiPiero and Pat McManus wrote a song that became a good-sized hit for the Oak Ridge Boys. They were happy with their hit and had absolutely no reason to believe at the time they wrote it that Miller Beer would buy the rights to use the song in a long media campaign. But Miller Beer did, and DiPiero and McManus made money beyond their

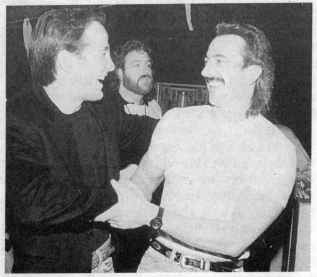

Aaron Tippin clowns with Clint Black backstage.

wildest dreams for their little song about their baby who is "American Made."

Similarly, when Aaron Tippin and Buddy Brock wrote "You've Got To Stand For Something," they were thinking about character, about being your own man, about having values that do not fall in the face of fads and peer pressure. They wrote it long before Iraq invaded Kuwait.

When we sent our troops to the Middle East, they must have wondered if the American public would remain behind them, or turn on them the way so many had done to our military people during the Vietnam War. When Aaron Tippin performed for the Desert Storm troops with Bob Hope, the song hit home out there in the desert. It spoke directly to them, saying, "What we are doing is right, and *that* is what is important." Hope's TV special carried the message back home, and for just a little while, at least as long as CNN's cameras were focused on the Gulf War, much of America forgot its obsession with possessions and thought about deeds.

Just a short, inspiring moment in the history of the United States, and of country music. Then America went back to everyday survival. In the meantime, however, young Aaron Tippin was a star, and Nashville's Music Row was soon split between those who thought Tippin was a one-album wonder, and those who thought that Tippin was on the road to major country hunkhood.

He certainly seemed to qualify for hunkhood. A South Carolina native still in his early thirties, his biceps and pecs bulged from years of determined bodybuilding. Both his voice and his image, that of the late-nineteenth-century mustached man who stood for something, were striking. He even had a palmetto tattooed on his right arm and was a qualified commercial aircraft pilot. One of the *Nashville Tennessean*'s two stellar country music writers referred to Tippin's music as "uncompromising, in-your-face hillbilly music . . . yowling, moaning-the-blues, dirt-floor, hard-core, by-god Country with a capital 'C'." Tippin's first review in *USA Today*, in December of 1990, offered a bit of prophecy from David Zimmerman: "This South Carolina native has that rare ability to sound totally swallowed up by his songs, and his unabashedly high, yodel-y vocals will remind many of Hank Williams, Sr. This guy is the big discovery of 1991."

"You've Got To Stand For Something" was a hit country single apart from the Gulf War, but RCA managed to get a lot of career-building publicity for Aaron out of the Bob Hope event. For a little while he was being carried in all sorts of major media, then his fifteen minutes as a media celebrity were over, and he continued with the serious business of becoming a country music star.

As they say in Hollywood, cut to the spring of 1992. Aaron has a number one hit single called "There Ain't Nothin' Wrong With The Radio." It's different, it's fun, it's Tippin, and it's propelling his album sales as if it were a booster jet.

The new album, *Read Between The Lines,* entered the *Billboard* top 200 album chart, which includes pop and everybody else, in the number seventy-seven position and by this time was nearly top ten on the country album charts. For Aaron Tippin it begins to look as though the Desert Storm hoopla was just a casual introduction to the world of country stardom. *Read Between The Lines* is the real thing. Back at the end of 1990, David Zimmerman had it right.

In the 1960s and seventies, California was responsible for a big chunk of country music action. Buck Owens, Merle Haggard, Susan Raye, Kenny Rogers, Emmylou Harris, Linda Ronstadt, and other country stars cut many country hits on the West Coast. Nashville had always felt just a bit insecure about its position as country music capital because, after all, Los Angeles was America's entertainment capital, with plenty of media and money to publicize and emphasize its accomplishments in country music.

But in the late seventies, things began to change. Rodney Crowell and Rosanne Cash, Emmylou, Vince Gill, and a number of talented songwriters, producers, and music business figures moved to Middle Tennessee, and as the prestige of Nashville's major label offices increased within their companies, the possibilities of West Coast artists becoming country stars while maintaining their L.A. base have diminished. That is not to say that L.A. will not rise again in the world of country music. It surely will. But today, among all the major record-selling young country acts, only the iconoclastic Dwight Yoakam consistently records in southern California.

Although Dwight Yoakam is from Kentucky and Ohio, his early Nashville experiences were not among the best days of his life. After he went to California and found success, he was widely quoted in a number of magazines about his adverse attitude toward Music City. Nevertheless, his recording career is carefully nurtured by the sales and promotion people in the Warner/Reprise offices in Nashville. One of his closest associates in Nashville is promotion executive Nick Hunter, who had some interesting things to say about Yoakam.

''With the exception of Garth Brooks,'' he says, ''who I have met but don't know, I would say that Dwight Yoakam is probably the smartest country artist I've ever been around. He has a real good view and idea of what he really is. . . . He came up with this whole marketing scheme; look, what you have is pretty much himself and, you know it's worked. Also, Dwight's selling a lot of records and he hasn't worked

Dwight Yoakam

the road [concerts, personal appearances, around the country, etc.] in about two years.''

Even without road appearances his current album, *If There Was A Way*, is far beyond gold status. In fact, it is number two among current Warner Brothers albums, according to Hunter.

What does he do if he's not on the road, as all good country artists are supposed to be?

"He stays home, spends money, stays on his ranch," says Hunter. "Drives around L.A., goofs around. Becoming a celebrity is driving him crazy because he's getting calls all the time from these grocery store magazines wanting to know about him."

Yoakam is less likely to come out with the acid public quotes that once made him so controversial, says Hunter.

"What happened was that the first time he started saying all these things it never dawned on him that people really paid attention to him. When he [criticized CBS Records for dropping Johnny Cash] he made [the comment] to some European [British] newspaper and it got back over here, he was just astounded that people printed what he said."

So, says Hunter, he is naturally a little more cautious about who he talks to and what he says.

"You know, he doesn't eat meat and he just signed a six-figure deal with McDonald's to do a commercial. . . he's putting up their salads and all the other stuff and not mentioning any kind of meat or any other thing that he wouldn't eat there. He called yesterday, and they're supposed to shoot the commercial over the weekend I believe; they asked him if he would drive his—cause he drives an old Cadillac—if he'd drive it through the Golden Arches for the commercial. He said no! He says, 'I'm not gonna do that!' He's been asked and has refused any kind of beer, or cigarette, or tobacco endorsements; he writes most of his own songs, is very interested in giving his listeners value on his CD; *If There Was A Way* has fourteen cuts on it [compared to the usual

Dwight Yoakam with hero Buck Owens

number of ten]. A very principled, idealistic young guy.''

So why would such a principled, idealistic young guy who could live anywhere he wants live in a place like L.A., with its association with greed and fast bucks?

''He's an odd creature; he likes to go and look around and in L.A. you can do that any time of the day or night.... [but] he used to be able to go around with either a baseball hat on or a leather jacket and no hat and people wouldn't recognize him but in the last six months it's gotten a lot crazier... But he just likes it out there. He likes the weather, he likes the people and, one thing Dwight says, 'I don't like the politics of the music business and living in Nashville, if you're an entertainer, you cannot get away from it.' ''

One of the ways country singers living in Nashville get known is by singing on publishers' demos. Publishers' demos are studio recordings of songs that publishers pitch to singers and producers. The ultimate goal, of course, is a hit record, or at least a good album cut.

Since publishers' demos are first and foremost a sales tool, the publishers and writers of the song want to hire the best pickers and singers they can afford in order to make the best demo. Every so often a great singer comes along who does not yet have a record deal. Some songwriter or publisher hears his voice and hires him to sing on his demo. Then the word spreads and soon the singer has all the work he can handle. He's grateful for the money because he's accustomed to not having any, but he's also frustrated because even though so many publishers and songwriters are anxious to use him on their demos, none of the record companies are willing to risk their money making *real* records with him. If our demo singer is also a songwriter, he is additionally frustrated by the fact that many of the songs he demos go on to get recorded, yet nobody seems to want to record *his* songs in spite of the fine demos he makes of them.

For a couple of years Joe Diffie was one of the busiest demo singers on Nashville's Music Row. As Joe told Jack Hurst in the *Chicago Tribune*, ''I started off singing demos of a couple of songs that I wrote. And a couple of other musicians were there and they said, 'Hey, I want to get you to do one of *my* songs.'

Joe Diffie (left) and Mark Chesnutt goofin' for the camera.

Or they referred me to other people: "I heard this guy sing this song the other day, and he did good.'

"After about a year I was singing more demos than I could keep up with. Every day I did four or five."

This went on for month after month. And some of the songs Joe demoed became hits *by* other people *for* other people. But Joe was not terribly discouraged because he has a lot of confidence in his ability—some have suggested that he's downright cocky—and because he was aware that "how far you get doesn't necessarily have to do with how much talent you have. It's who's got the most want-to.''

Joe Diffie—FanFair '92.

Oklahoma-born, Joe Diffie's dad is the kind of man who isn't afraid to try his hand at something new and put his heart into it. He's been a teacher, a farmer, a coach, a truckdriver, and a welder. Men like that often pass on to their sons the courage to take measured risks in their lives. So young Joe did not worry about failure as he set out to build a music career by playing the VFWs and honky-tonks. He married young and supported his family by working in a foundry by day. Nineteen eighty-six was a turning point. The foundry closed down and so did his marriage. At the age of twenty-seven he left Duncan, Oklahoma, and headed for the Camelot of the South, Nashville, Tennessee.

December is a bad month to start a Nashville music career. The days are short and the nights are cold and

Music Row is so preoccupied with round after round of Christmas parties that they seldom have a moment to give to the new kid in town. Diffie found work at the Gibson Guitar Company and spent his spare time making friends in the music business. One of them, songwriter Tim Mensy, was doing a lot of demo singing; but when he was signed to a CBS recording contract he had to give up the demo game. He began referring much of his work to Diffie, and Joe made the most of it.

It's surprising that successful demo singers are able to avoid destroying their voices. They have to take work when it's offered or they may lose the account. That can mean nine or more hours of session work on the busy days. But Joe got through it, doing much of his demo singing at Tree Publishing Company. Tree is owned by Sony. CBS Records is owned by Sony. They are sister companies. CBS heard a lot about Diffie's singing, so it wasn't a complete surprise when they signed him to an Epic recording deal.

Diffie's first release, "Home," became the first single to make it to the number one position on the country charts in both *Radio & Records* and the highly regarded *Gavin Report* for more than one week. His career has been at full tilt ever since. Four number one singles came from his album *A Thousand Winding Roads* and there are sure to be more on the way.

For quite a few years now the hottest demo singer in Nashville has been John Wesley Ryles. At the age of seventeen, a couple of decades ago, John Wesley had a country hit record called "Kay," and quite a few years later he had a major record deal that brought him a number of solid chart singles without bringing him huge sales acclaim. John Wesley is a nice looking fellow with the kind of personality everybody likes. It's nothing short of amazing that despite the fact that the Nashville publishing business believes so strongly in his ability to ''sell'' a song on a demo tape, he has not had a record deal in some time. The public should get another chance to appreciate John Wesley Ryles the way the music publishing industry appreciates him.

Every so often you get a guy that everybody in the business knows is great. The whole business roots for him, radio plays him, he gets number one records, but the public doesn't buy his albums. And everybody in the business knows why.

Steve Wariner is such a guy. He moves Music Row with his singing and knocks everybody out with his guitar playing. He has demonstrated his songwriting virtuosity again and again. In short, he has done everything that makes a star except cross that magic line between hit radio music and people music. Hit radio is what program directors believe people feel comfortable with when they're driving a car and people music is the music that moves people from their home to Tower or Wal-Mart to buy albums and make the music their own.

Steve has been on a number of record labels and has had big radio records on several of them, so when Arista Records signed him a short while back, Music Row wished him well, but they weren't making any bets. The title of his first Arista album, *I Am Ready*, may have reflected the hope that at long last he had gained that little extra something that would finally push him over the hump.

He had. That extra something was an old Bill Anderson classic called ''Tips Of My Fingers.'' It's a beautiful country ballad with a hit past but no definitive cut on it until Steve Wariner took it into the studio and showed that he was what few really thought he was, a very good *country* singer.

If "Tips Of My Fingers" should make Steve Wariner's career that would be poetic justice because Steve has had country stardom at the tips of his fingers for years. Yes, he started playing professionally while still a child in Indiana, where Dottie West discovered him playing in an Indianapolis club. He toured with her for three years as her bass player, stayed on the road a while longer, then his friend, session-legend Paul Yandell, introduced him to Chet Atkins. In 1980, Atkins signed Steve to his first recording contract. He's been on the verge of stardom ever since. Maybe his time is near.

The record producer is the guy who oversees recording sessions. Typically, he will hire the musicians, have a strong voice in which songs will be recorded, determine the musical sound of the session, be a vocal coach to the artist during the session, and make vital decisions on the final mix of the recording.

Nashville has known some great producers, from Owen Bradley, Chet Atkins, and Billy Sherrill in days gone by to present talents like James Stroud, Jim Ed Norman, Kyle Lehning, Tony Brown, Barry Beckett, and Garth Fundis. But the best producer in the history of Nashville recorded music might be Allen Reynolds. Reynolds was responsible for many of Crystal Gayle's greatest hits, some of Emmylou Harris, much of Kathy Mattea, and all of Garth Brooks. Allen Reynolds *is* musical integrity.

Now there's Hal Ketchum, one of Allen's latest projects. People in the South and West think that the state of New York is paved solid from the Hudson River to the Great Lakes, but Hal Ketchum was born and raised in Greenwich, New York, a tiny town near the Vermont border. Thus his first single on Curb Records, "Small Town Saturday Night," spoke about a world he knew, and he carried it all the way to the number one slot on the *Billboard* country singles chart.

Hal's dad was an old banjo picker and his grandfather was a concert violinist who moved to a small town and started fiddling at square dances. Like nearly all the other artists in this chapter, Ketchum was performing in clubs long before he was old enough to drink in them, and like nearly all the rest of them, he knew his country but also liked rock 'n roll.

He was a drummer and spent years in Florida and Texas, drumming. While living in central Texas he began to garner inspiration from songwriter/artists like Lyle Lovett and Townes Van Zandt. Then he started performing in Austin and visiting Nashville, his eye fixed on an artist's career. He cut an album in 1986 for an independent label and signed with a publishing company that liked his singing and songwriting and helped him go after a record deal. A few years later he had that deal, with Curb Records, and almost immediately the deal turned into a number one smash.

The album, *Past The Point of Rescue*, is past the point of concern about its success. In 1992 it hit top ten on the country album chart, and achieved gold status, solid evidence that Hal Ketchum is a clear candidate for hot country hunkdom.

In the seventies a dark young man from Brooklyn moved his business and domicile to Nashville and Music Row hasn't been the same since. His name is Ron Haffkine, and his business was the management and production of Dr. Hook, one of America's foremost pop groups. Everybody knows that pop groups have no business in Nashville, and Nashville has no business doing pop groups. Or at least that's the rep that New York and L.A. have managed to stick on Nashville since the sixties. Surely Ron Haffkine was not born to be a son of the South. He had the impatient, irascible temperament of a New Yorker and it took time for him and laid back Nashville to adjust to each other.

But Haffkine knew that Nashville was a great place to find songs, and he also knew that the studios and musicians in Nashville were perfect for what he was doing with Dr. Hook. For a number of years he produced big hits with Hook, and then he retired. By the time he decided to come back it was clear he had learned a great deal about the new traditional country music, so few people were surprised when Haffkine hit the charts hard with a marvelous debut album by Davis Daniel on Mercury/Polygram titled *Fighting Fire With Fire*.

Raised poor in Montana and Nebraska, and then Denver, Davis dreamed of music early but got started much later than most of the prodigies in the field. He didn't begin working on his C, F, and G chords until he was seventeen, but he learned fast and soon he was picking in a local pizza parlor. After a time he graduated to being the leader of a band, the Davis Daniel Band, in fact, and they were a hot country unit in

Denver. Many singers who become local country heroes puff up their feathers and stay put rather than risk failure by trying for the big time, but Davis had the fever.

"I thought that I had to go," he later told his label biographer. "Otherwise, I knew that when I turned forty, I'd kick my butt for not trying it."

So he came to Nashville and drove a beer truck by day and played the open mikes and writers' nights by night. One night he was spotted by a label executive who had come to see somebody else. A lawyer he knew suggested that Daniel meet with Haffkine for some showbiz advice. They met, Daniel played Haffkine a tape, and a hit-making career began. Sometimes it all seems so very simple, just as long as you don't bother to count the times he sang on an open mike night when a record executive did *not* come.

More than anybody else, Marty Stuart represents the things that make so many of the young country hotshots what they are. On the one hand, Marty's image is that of the hillbilly rocker—in fact, one of his biggest records to date was his 1991 hit, *Hillbilly Rock*. But that doesn't make him any less country. In fact, Stuart has one of the most impeccably country backgrounds of any artist in the business today.

Mississippi-born, he was a mandolin and guitar virtuoso early enough in life to hit the road with Lester Flatt at the age of thirteen. After Flatt's death in 1979, Marty started to expand his musical interests, picking up many of his influences from the old Sun Records rockabilly days. He played a strange, unclassifiable bluegrass-type music with fiddler Vassar Clements, worked with the great guitarist Doc Watson, and did

Country rocker Marty Stuart

six years on the road with Johnny Cash. Many music people knew about Marty and respected him, but he didn't start working hard on his singing style until his first major record deal with CBS in 1986. That deal didn't work out very well but he just kept on working at his craft. Two years later he signed with MCA and recorded his *Hillbilly Rock* album, which brought him three radio hits in quick succession.

During the past year Marty has been touring with fellow hillbilly rocker Travis Tritt, and the association couldn't have hurt Marty very much because in the summer MCA released his *This One*'s *Gonna Hurt You* album. It hit the country album charts at the number fourteen position and the *Billboard* 200 pop charts at number ninety-one. It's fairly obvious that *This One*'s *Gonna Hurt You* is the album that's going to help propel Marty Stuart to stardom. He is building a recording career on a firm foundation. "What I have a passion to do," he says, "is to take what I've learned and been a part of in the past with all the masters and bridge it into the future. I'm crusading for hillbilly music."

Billy Dean may or may not be a country crusader, but he is one of the hunkier hunks out there, and one of country's most exciting up-and-comers. A Florida native, Dean's dad had a band and while still in his tender years, Billy was playing in it. In the early eighties he won a Wrangler Starsearch talent contest and shortly thereafter moved to Nashville.

When someone moves to Nashville to be in the music business, the first big question is how to support oneself while trying to do what one came to do. Some load trucks. Some drive them. Some wait tables or make them in a factory. Billy put together a touring band and started traveling, opening shows for Mel Tillis and Ronnie Milsap, among others.

Enter Jimmy Gilmer. You might recognize that name if your music memory goes back as far as 1963. Jimmy Gilmer and the Fireballs had one of the top pop hits of that year, "Sugar Shack." There are a number of old rock 'n rollers who eventually settled down in the Nashville music business. In addition to Gilmer, they include Jimmy Bowen, who started out as a hit-making singer with Buddy Knox and the Rhythm Orchids and eventually became the most powerful man in the Nashville record business; Johnny Cymbal, who had a big hit with "Mr. Bassman" three decades ago, and wound up in Nashville writing country songs; Bruce Chanel, who had a smash with "Hey Baby" way back when and today writes songs in Nashville; and a guy named Conway Twitty, an Elvis-sounding rock 'n roller in the late fifties who went on to have more than fifty number one country hits.

Gilmer is a quiet, shy, nice man who has become one of Nashville's more respected publishing executives. He signed Billy Dean to a songwriting deal with EMI Music and then talked Capitol Nashville/SBK Records into a giving Dean a recording contract. Before long, the talented kid had had an impressive number of songs recorded by artists that included Ronnie Milsap and Randy Travis, and in 1990 Capitol released his debut album, *Young Man*.

During the winter the Nashville music industry holds its annual Country Radio Seminar for the country radio industry. Often the high point of the seminar is the "New Faces Show," during which nine or ten of country's most impressive new acts strut their stuff for country's top radio programmers. The stakes are high. It's a great opportunity for an act to give radio a face to go with the voice they've been playing—or not playing—on the air. If you're good on the "New Faces Show," you can give your career a power boost. On the 1991 "New Faces Show," Billy Dean was great. Billy's early single, "Somewhere In My Broken Heart," landed high on the charts and "Only Here For A Little While" made it all the way to number one.

Although now is a time for traditional sounding country singers, the more mainstream sounds of Billy Dean have found a home on country radio. Many believe that the big sales figures that mark a superstar are so close that he can almost reach out and touch them. In the summer of 1992 Billy Dean delivered a smash hit called "Billy The Kid," that propelled his *Billy Dean* album up both the country and the pop charts. Watch this guy. More important, listen to him. He's part of country music's dazzling future.

The next hunk grew up reaching out and touching people, then enfolding them and crushing them. Many of the men who read this book already know that Mike Reid was an All-American defensive tackle at Penn State, then All-Pro with the Cincinnati Bengals.

I wonder how many of them know just how ornery you have to be to be an All-Pro defensive tackle? You have to be a very bad boy. You have to want to punish people, not necessarily maim them but at least smash them hard enough for them to wish the next morning that they had taken up ballroom dancing.

That must have been another Mike Reid. *This* Mike Reid plays piano with sensitive fingers, sings songs with a sensitive voice, and writes them with a sensitive heart.

And his football career is behind him. *Way* behind him. Music is his vocation and his passion. Some say that serious people are the happiest people. They're too involved with what they're doing to require the diversion that brings laughter. Mike has been serious about music at least since he heard his first classical piece at the age of thirteen. He majored in music at Penn State, had a short, very successful career in the National Football League, and retired at twenty-seven.

Now, why would a great football player retire at twenty-seven? Well, considering what professional football does to the knees, shoulders, and ankles, not to mention the *fingers* (ever wonder why linemen tape their hands?) a sensible piano player might well ask what sense it makes to continue playing the game.

He retired and began a career performing in small venues with a band and trying to write songs. That's a long way down from the physical release and mass public acclaim that he had known, but Mike was faithful, and nearly a decade after his last bit of mayhem on the football field, he had his first number one hit, "Inside," recorded by Ronnie Milsap. Since then his songwriting career has been consistently successful and his songs have been quality all the way, as evidenced by the Grammy for "Stranger In My House," and two more fistfuls of number one records.

Nineteen ninety-one was definitely not the right time for a big, bespectacled introspective Yankee to go after a country recording career, but Mike must not have known that because his CBS single "Walk On Faith" hit the number one spot on the country singles charts and radio has been playing it ever since. Next time you hear it—and you will if you listen to country stations—listen to it carefully and you will hear the character of the man shining through the record, crystal clear, a kind, decent, gentle man fortunate enough to be spending his life doing the things he loves best.

Another CBS recording artist with a brilliant future is Collin Raye. I mentioned before that Dwight Yoakam is the only major country star recording in California, but that's a bit of a half-truth. Collin Raye, who certainly appears to be on the road to major stardom, split the recording of his first CBS album, *All I Can Be*, between Nashville and Los Angeles. Collin is a fan of studio musicians. His album liner notes show a collection that includes some of the best from both cities.

Collin himself has been a musician since the age of seven, when he played tambourine and sang harmony with his brother Scott. His mother had been a singer in Collin's home state of Arkansas; it was never a question if he was going to be a performer, only a question of where. In the early eighties it looked as if the where would be Oregon. Then Collin and Scott went on to Reno, Nevada, where they played the casinos for good money, always a rare commodity in the performing business.

Somebody heard them and got them a recording deal in Nashville with Mercury Records. Before the group could really get off the ground the old regime vanished from the label and so did the group. Collin learned the first time around that an artist can't depend on others to make things happen.

When his next break came along in the form of a solo deal with Epic Records, Collin Raye was prepared. The old saying, or cliché, is that success is where preparation meets opportunity. His first Epic album, *All I Can Be*, is a top ten country album with a solid position among the pop top one hundred albums. The title single was a chart-topper. *USA Today*'s Dave Zimmerman tells us that "his is one of the strongest, most comfortable male voices Nashville has come up with in a while." Collin Raye is an overnight success—just a quarter of a century since the first time he sang harmonies and smacked a tambourine performing with his brother.

3

Group Hunks

IN THE BEGINNING, STRING BANDS, WESTERN SWING bands, and bluegrass bands made a lot of the music we now call country. Their day faded and for many years the gospel-tinged Statler Brothers were the only consistent hit-making group in the world of country music. What had happened to the idea that a number of individuals with common musical goals could combine under a group identity and thereby achieve fame and fortune?

For one thing, rock happened, sixties counterculture rock that grew hair and praised sex, drugs, and incivility. Southern and rural folk were more repelled by that image than their urban counterparts, and to them one of the premier communicators of that image was the rock group. Some of these groups, such as the Byrds, Rolling Stones, Pure Prairie League, the Eagles, the Flying Burrito Brothers, and Poco bore a heavy country influence, but country fans were wary of subversion, so few country radio stations played even the most country offerings presented by these groups.

The sixties and early seventies rolled by without a

strong country music group debut. And then along came Larry Gatlin. A fine songwriter and singer, Gatlin relied heavily on the marvelous blended harmonies of his brothers Rudy and Steve, but his experience must have convinced him that the group image was a handicap. He had three or four years of hits as a solo act before he changed the name on the label to "Larry Gatlin and the Gatlin Brothers Band."

By this time there was another group on the scene, one with a three decade history in the gospel world. The Oak Ridge Boys were restless and ambitious, and hip to a variety of hit sounds, from middle-of-the-road country to old time rock 'n roll. Together they rode a hit country song called "Y'all Come Back Saloon" to the top of the singles charts and they have been country stars ever since.

But one more group barrier remained to fall. There were still no self-contained groups who played their own instruments as well as singing harmonies. In 1981 such a group finally arrived, and they happened to be the only new act to break into country radio during an otherwise fairly depressing country music year. Alabama recorded a mix of happy, fiddle-driven songs about the joys of country living and pretty love ballads with results unprecedented in the history of country groups. Soon there were a dozen more chart-busting groups, but none of them could come close to the incredible sales figures generated by these four down-home boys. And to this day, Alabama is the king of country groups. Although their album sales may not be what they were at the group's peak, in the spring of 1992 they were back at the top of the country singles charts with "Born Country." They have a gold album on the country album charts and they can still draw huge numbers of excited fans to their concerts.

Let's meet some of their challengers.

Country music has its share of mythic heroes, including cowboys, farmers, "working men," and truck drivers. Truck drivers, in turn, have their mythic trucks, among which one of the most mythic is the Diamond Reo. So it's appropriate that somewhere along the way a country group would come along that would choose to call itself Diamond Reo.

But they didn't. The name of the group is Diamond Rio, because, says lead singer Marty Roe in an interview with country music writer Jack Hurst, "I kind of thought it was spelled that way."

No matter how they spell their name, Diamond Rio is hot, and getting hotter. Their album, *Diamond Rio*, is well past a year on the country album charts, having gone gold, and their single, "Mama Don't Forget To Pray For Me," enjoyed a trip high up on the singles charts. Their first single, "Meet In The Middle," was a number one smash and they've been special to radio and record-buyers ever since.

Diamond Rio, like a number of other country artists, started their career together as fresh-faced, enthusiastic, energetic young performers at Opryland, Nashville's famous music theme park. In those days they called themselves the Grizzly River Boys because the park had a ride called the Grizzly River Rampage.

Later, as the Tennessee River Boys, their road schedule had more twists and turns in it than the river they were named after. When they weren't on the road trying to break even they were doing lawn care work to make a living. In the meantime, they were striving desperately for a recording contract, the only way they could get out of their slavelike life-style.

Marty Roe had attended David Lipscomb University in Nashville with Monty Powell, who had embarked upon a songwriting career at about the same time the Tennessee River Boys were forsaking the security of Opryland for the uncertain misery of anonymous road travel. Powell eventually became associated with record executive Tim DuBois, and the three developed a musical relationship. DuBois saw the group perform as an opening act for George Jones. That inspired him to take some of the group's tapes to his associates at Arista Records. Soon there was a recording contract in the works, but nobody was particularly crazy about the name of the group, which sounded to some ears like a gospel name. It took months to come up with a new name. One of the rejects was T-Town Mavericks.

The group members are lead singer Marty Roe, who was named for Marty Robbins and leans toward the traditional; Gene Johnson, mandolin player and Dana Williams, bass player, both of whom love to sing those tight bluegrass harmonies; drummer Brian Prout, a rock 'n roller; and Dan Truman, a keyboard player with jazz in his bloodstream. The mixture of wills and influences in this band gives it a country basis with a refreshingly different musical undercurrent. They've shared adversity for years and now they are surely ready for the prosperity that comes from making hit records.

When a solo artist gets a record deal, he or she

generally just keeps his or her own name. But when an unknown group gets a deal, the group name becomes a matter of concern to the whole record company. Everybody wants to get into the act of finding a name that fits the image the group is trying to project. As a longtime working group, Diamond Rio went through several names before their Arista deal sent them searching seriously for a name that would suit their recording image.

BNA's new hit group, the Remingtons, had no name at all at the time they got their label deal, and to make things more vague and odd, even their label didn't have a name.

Founding members Jimmy Griffin, Richard Mainegra, and Rick Yancey can claim three-quarters of a century of music business experience among them and yet their vocal signature may be the most refreshing in country music today. Louisiana native Mainegra, and Yancey, who is from Memphis, were founding members of the pop group Cymarron, which hit only once, back in 1971, with "Rings." The group didn't last too long after their hit, and Mainegra moved to Nashville.

Condensed into a short record label bio, Mainegra's stay in Nashville looks like a happy tale of success. His songwriting garnered hit records by Elvis Presley ("Separate Ways"), Tanya Tucker ("Here's Some Love"), and Tom Bresh ("Home Made Love"), and his incomparable voice made him one of Nashville's most successful jingle singers. But then there were the hundreds of songs that didn't get recorded—every songwriter has those—and there were record deals that were supposed to happen but didn't.

Meanwhile Yancey was going through the same

mixture of success and frustration playing guitar on recording sessions for Willie Nelson, Waylon Jennings, the Atlanta Rhythm Section, and Johnny Cash, among others.

Jimmy Griffin was a key member of the major pop group Bread. After Bread disbanded, Griffin went back home to Memphis and recorded a number of album projects. Then he worked with a country group called Black Tie, which in 1990 had a fairly successful country single called "Learning The Game."

By then, Mainegra, Yancey, and Griffin were pooling their songwriting talents, and probably considering the idea of recording together.

RCA's Nashville head of A & R, Josh Leo, heard the three, with their bright acoustic guitar sound and their flawless harmonies, at a friend's house. Josh got RCA president Joe Galante all excited about them and they were slated for a deal with RCA's new, unnamed subsidiary. Now came some waiting, something that each member of the group had become quite used to in their combined seventy-five years in the music business. The label got organized, and then it got named, and in the process the group came up with and rejected any number of names for themselves before some sensitive soul suggested the name Remingtons, which has a wonderful connection to explosive firepower as well as a solid sound to it. Just say it: "Rem-ing-tons." Anyway, their first single, "A Long Time Ago," was powerful enough to go top ten.

Do you ever wonder how seriously artists take record reviews? Read this:

"We were flying to San Francisco," reports Mainegra. "Part of a promotional tour, and we were all excited because our first record was doing great. They're passing around the magazines, and one of them has a review on us, so we can't wait to get it open and see all those great things they're writing about us, because up to then the reviews had been good.

"She tore us apart! Something like, 'The Remingtons are more like cap guns.' And worse. By the time we landed in San Francisco, we were almost in tears."

Speaking of reviews, country music's most famous reviewer is Robert K. Oermann, who is also one of the most knowledgeable of all country journalists. Oermann reviews for the highly respected Nashville publication *Music Row*. His reviews are not always kind, but they are always honest. A sample comment, unkind but knowledgeable: "They put a blindfold on her, stuffed her ears with cotton, and laughed while she tried to play Pin the Tail on the Melody in the studio." Another: "Get out the Dristan: We're talking serious nasality here. So serious that the congestion has affected his hearing and pitch."

But when Oermann hears something he loves, he will give his heart completely. Thus, his comment on the Remingtons' debut single, "A Long Time Ago": "Absolute ecstasy. Harmonies to die for. Heavenly mandolin. What more on earth could you ask for in a record. Love it. Love it. Love it. Love it. Love it. PLEASE make them stars."

So far the Remingtons are on track to stardom, which should please Bob Oermann.

Warner/Reprise Records is a powerhouse in Nashville. They started the latest country explosion when they started selling millions of Randy Travis records. They brought cowpunk to the top of the charts with Dwight Yoakam and when they found Travis Tritt they developed his career with the sure-footed confidence that comes from their leader, Jim Ed Norman, and filters down through the ranks.

Without hype, letting the music speak for itself, Warner/Reprise has now given us a country group called Little Texas. Their first single, "Some Guys Have All The Love," was a top ten record, and the video of the same song went to number one on the Nashville Network chart. A couple of months later, their brand new album hit the *Billboard* 200 Top Albums chart at position one hundred thirty-three, a spectacular entry for a new group.

The *Dallas Morning News* described the group as having the "hard rock edge and harmonies reminiscent of the early Eagles." Although the group has Texas roots, they took their name from an area south of Nashville, fabled for its law-defying rednecks back in the forties and fifties. Male country groups seem to lean toward names that evoke sociopathic or antiestablishment pursuits (Kentucky Headhunters, Pirates of the Mississippi, and, you might recall, T-Town Mavericks).

Little Texas consists of Tim Rushlow, lead singer, guitar and mandolin player, from Arlington, Texas; Dwayne O'Brien, a guitarist from Oklahoma with a degree in chemistry; Porter Howell, a Texas guitarist who works out most of the group's musical arrangements; Duane Propes, bass player from Texas who dotes on the classics as well as classic country; Brady Seals, from Ohio, kin to songwriting great Troy Seals and the golden-throated Dan Seals; and drummer Del Gray, another Ohioan—generally biographers don't have much to say about a band's drummers.

Unlike solo artists, bands strive for a sound that evolves out of the collective interests and abilities of the various members. In order for that sound to come together the band has to play an awful lot of music. In 1991 alone Little Texas played about three hundred dates all over the country. They tried to find places to play that were near important radio stations, and then the label tried to make sure the DJs would get out to hear Little Texas in the smaller clubs. If you can get the DJs to do that, suddenly the group takes on an identity more powerful than just the sound of a new record coming out of a studio monitor.

One of the hot promotional formats in show business in recent years has been the talent contest—"You Can Be A Star," "Star Search," this talent contest, that songwriter competition. To complicate things, some of these contests are strictly money-making scams for the promoters, while others can be a pathway to career success.

Oklahoman Ronnie Dunn was a music professional with a band, a club to play in, and otherwise not much in career prospects, when his drummer walked into a convenience store in Tulsa and saw the display and entry blanks for a talent contest sponsored by Marlboro. Jamie Oldaker must have had very little to do with his time, for he mailed in one of Ronnie's demo tapes.

Dunn won.

He won a nice cash price and lots of recording studio time, but that's not the amazing part. The amazing part was that Scott Hendricks, the engineer on the sessions at that studio, was close enough to Tim DuBois, head of Arista Records in Nashville, to play the tapes for Tim. Tim got Ronnie together with Kix Brooks, a highly respected Nashville songwriter and vocalist. His advice to them may go down in the chronicles of Nashville legend. ''Keep your boots on,'' he said, ''keep your jeans on and keep it country.''

He was telling two very versatile music people where their roots were and where their bread was buttered. Both of them had experienced more than their share of disappointments in the music business—no, that's not quite correct. In the music business there is no such thing as ''more than their share.'' Both had had plenty of disappointments, so they were both ready to make the most of opportunities that came their way.

What came their way was a couple of number one singles right out of the box, ''Brand New Man,'' and ''My Next Broken Heart,'' and a tremendous followup single titled ''Neon Moon.'' Their album, Brand New Man, made top five country and has gone gold but, more amazing, has zoomed into the top twenty on the Billboard 200 album charts. The major reason for this is ''Boot Scootin' Boogie,'' which took a fast ride to the top of Billboard's country charts and became one of the hotter singles on the pop charts in the month of August.

Which brings us to an interesting trend in country music. If you turn on CMT and watch country music videos, you'll discover that dancing has become an important part of country entertainment. Actually, it's always been there. The Grand Ole Opry has featured clogging acts for decades. Texas music in general and western swing in particular have always been dance-oriented. And this past spring, when the "Achy Breaky Heart" explosion was built around a dance, it was obvious that dancing had attained a new level of importance in country music. "Boot Scootin' Boogie" is a dance record, and Brooks and Dunn are on their way to the top of their profession.

So by now you know enough to tell your friends that, no, Brooks and Dunn are not Garth Brooks and Holly Dunn, and if you've been listening to country radio at all, you understand that these guys have a sound built on great songs and tight harmonies.

How to describe their music? One talented journalist has called it "a revved-up brand of honky-tonk music that sparkles with wit, intelligence and instrumental fire. Their first LP roars through a landscape of hot dresses and cold beers, where flirtation and heartbreak chase each other around smoky dance halls, and life and love have a compressed Saturday night urgency to them." Sounds a lot like the sage advice from wise and friendly A & R chief Tim DuBois.

Grand candidates for the wildest band in country music are still the Kentucky Headhunters.

Record labels often hire free-lance writers to create short biographic pieces about their artists. Most of these pieces are fairly straightforward, unexciting fact statements; but every so often, when the subject is of special interest, the biographer will get creative. So opens the Headhunters' Mercury/Polygram bio:

"Their name suggests a band of wild pigmies stalking the hills of Appalachia, the local folk afraid to go out at night lest a blowgun find its target, and their shrunken heads fated to hang from the rear view mirror of a two-toned Chevy."

The *Gavin Report* also managed to wax lyrical: "Bluegrass in black leather. A curled-lip snarl, a barroom beat and an electric guitar slither, but a hillbilly heart." And *Stereo Review* remarked, "Wanton heathenism never sounded so good."

What all this means is that when the Kentucky Headhunters exploded on the country scene, they did so with an image so vivid that you couldn't fail to grasp what they were. Their first album, *Pickin' On Nashville*, went gold faster than any debut album by a group in country music history. Within a year it was platinum and is still selling.

And yet, the Kentucky Headhunters are distinctly out of sync with the rest of what is happening in country music. The heaviest hitters among country music acts do not carry around the image of arrogance so long associated with pop acts. The Kentucky Headhunters might attract the same crowds that loved Hank Williams, Jr., during those lonely years when Hank stirred up three-quarters of the excitement that country music had to offer. They took an old Bill Monroe tune called "Walk Softly On This Heart Of Mine" and rammed it down our throats with a southern rock flavor as strong as backwoods Kentucky sour mash whiskey, 140 proof. Country was just beginning to pick up the steam locomotive momentum we're all so comfortable with now. They let us know that country was in for an era of exciting unpredictability, and we'll always owe them that.

But will the Kentucky Headhunters endure? In 1992, two of their members departed from the group, and as yet nothing has happened that would reassure us of their survival. But even if their wild, raggedy sounds never again assail us, except as a manic echo of the past, we should be grateful to them for giving us energy and excitement at a time when country music needed it.

Would you believe that 1991 marked the tenth year of Sawyer Brown's existence? They were a red hot performing group long before they got their first record deal with Capitol—hot enough to win "Star Search." Their Capitol deal brought them immediate success, with hits like "Step That Step," "Betty's Bein' Bad," and "The Race Is On."

The ramrod of the group is hardworking Floridian Mark Miller, who sings lead and writes and coproduces so much of their music. The other members include Mark's old friend and cowriter Gregg Hubbard, who plays keyboard, bass player Jim Scholten, and drummer Joe Smyth. Gone from the group is big Bobby Randall, who has moved on to record production and television work. Sawyer Brown was so young when they first tasted success that even after a decade they still qualify for the name group-hunk.

And now a brief word on Shenandoah. What happened to them could happen to any group, but it shouldn't happen to a dog. A few years ago they caught everybody's attention with their *The Road Not Taken* album, which featured an incredibly wise and popular career record for the group called "Mama

Knows.'' They followed with three number one singles, and were obviously on their way to a successful group career. They had a fine country harmony sound and their lead singer, Marty Raybon, was blessed with the kind of voice that could steal the heart of anybody who had one.

It was exciting to look forward to the next Shenandoah record. But then complicated legal problems developed regarding the group's name. And for far too long, the sounds of Shenandoah disappeared from the airwaves.

They're back, with a chart-topping hit country single titled ''Rock My Baby.'' They were hot before and they have a good shot at being hot again. There's more group-hunk out there, of course. Confederate Railroad has just broken big on the Atlantic label. Restless Heart has been pumping out hits for years, and Pirates Of The Mississippi may steal their way to the top of the charts any day now. Nitty Gritty Dirt Band and Asleep At The Wheel are still making great music and the Texas Tornados are worth a lot more notice than they get from radio. Desert Rose Band is still in business, and sooner or later they are bound to start amassing the sales that their great harmonies deserve. There are some fine female groups and mixed groups out there too. Groups are now a major force in country music, and it looks as though they will be for a long time to come.

4

Garth Brooks

THE AMERICAN SOCIETY OF COMPOSERS, AUTHORS and Publishers was dedicating its sumptuous new quarters at the head of Nashville's Music Row. Although it was midday, many of country music's movers and shakers were on hand to see the new building and partake of the chicken and pasta buffet.

To add drama and panache to the occasion, ASCAP president Morton Gould presented an award to Garth Brooks in the glass enclosed ground floor conference room. Outside, in the rain, dozens of fans had their noses pressed against the glass to catch a glimpse. Inside, a couple of hundred music business people leaned forward to hear what Garth had to say.

Garth's acceptance speech was typical, not a speech at all, more like the sharing of an opinion or two with a couple of friends. He told them that ASCAP was the home of writers, and he was lucky to know so many fine writers. The right thing to say to an organization that represents songwriters, except that not a person in the room doubted that Garth Brooks meant what he said.

After the presentation was over, ASCAP's tough,

Garth Brooks in action!

smart chief counsel, Bernard Korman, turned to music publishing great Buddy Killen, with wonder in his eyes.

"Are they all as modest as he is?" he asked Buddy.

"Almost all," Buddy replied. "He is."

There is no reason to ask the obvious question, why is Garth Brooks as big a star as he is? The answer is that when an artist gets *that* big, nobody knows why. Currently Garth is selling about a million albums every month. His picture seems to be on the cover of every magazine.

I talked to Garth's management about an interview. Pam Lewis politely declined, citing overkill.

"It's not just the autobiography," she said—the

bidding among New York publishers reputedly had reached the seven figure mark. "There are three unauthorized biographies in progress right now." That was in addition to Michael McCall's quickie biography, which has been out for many months.

Everybody wants a piece of Garth. There isn't a songwriter in Nashville who wouldn't rather have an album cut by Garth than a single by almost anybody else. And almost every songwriter in Nashville has that opportunity, because even though the media publicizes Garth's songwriting prowess, he and his equally purist producer, Alan Reynolds, have their ears wide open for the next great song, no matter where it comes from.

In the world of country music, with its mighty entrenched record, publishing, and management moguls, Garth Brooks, the young man who only a few years ago was a wannabe just lingering around the newly opened offices of his comanager Bob Doyle, is the king if he wants to be.

But he doesn't appear to focus much on kingship. Garth Brooks wants to sing. He wants to write. He wants to entertain. He entrusts his business management to his managers, and he's fortunate or wise enough to have chosen people just as dedicated as he and Alan Reynolds.

Now, if all this sounds too good to be true, too bad. It is true. The music business may, or may not, be mired to its eyeballs in sleaze, but the Garth Brooks team's business is music. Let the personal life rumors fly, and they will. These people are determined to run fast enough to keep up with themselves.

What is the true story of Garth's rise from the guy

who wanted to entertain people to the hottest recording artist in music today, and the hottest selling country artist ever? A good place to start is with Jim Foglesong, who for many years was the most respected individual in the Nashville record industry. Jim, after all, is the man responsible for signing Garth Brooks to a Capitol recording contract.

"Bob Doyle," Foglesong remembers, "stopped me one day, I think he was in our building, and said, 'I'd like to see you for a minute.' I said, 'come on in.'

"He said, 'I signed a writer that I think might be an artist.' He said, 'This young feller from Oklahoma, Garth Brooks, I signed him strictly as a writer but he's been doing these writers' nights around town, and when he performs the crowd just goes crazy. . .and I would really value your opinion. . .I know you don't like to do live auditions in your office but, really, if you would just take enough time to let Garth bring his guitar in and do five or six numbers for you, I think you'd get a feeling—at least, I'd like to get your input.' "

You can feel Bob Doyle groping for the words, wanting to convey to Foglesong a sense of his own excitement, but Bob Doyle is not a hype artist, so he winds up doing a soft sell.

"I said, "Of course,' because Bob is a friend. He was right, I don't like—nobody likes to do auditions of that type but in this case, I did do it. I invited Lynn Schults, who was Vice President of A & R at Capitol, to come in.

"Garth came in and, we spoke; he obviously was somebody who had done some weightlifting and so forth and so we talked sports. . .and he told me about his scholarship at Oklahoma State in track and how he'd injured his knees playing football, a little small talk and then he picked up his guitar and he did I think six songs and I was so impressed with him. One of the reasons you don't like to do auditions in the office is that artists usually get extremely nervous— that's a very quiet, un-showbiz atmosphere and this is their big chance in the office of an executive and they get very uptight about it. The sound is not flattering to their voices at all, but Garth was not intimidated in any way. One particular song had some humor in it and he smiled and delivered the song with humor. . .all these songs were cowritten or written by

him and I was terrifically impressed. And when they left, I . . . told Lynn, that I'm ready to sign this guy now, and Lynn, who attended a lot more showcases than I did at that time, said, 'Well, he's good but you know, there are an awful lot of these guys around town—there's so much talent.' And I said, 'Well I know that but I think this guy *is* something special. I like the sound of his voice and I think he has tremendous writing potential.'

"And I said, 'You think about it but I'll tell you right now, you have my blessing to do something.'

" . . . we almost blew this because I had a lot of other things going on at the same time *but*, we had a staff meeting one Monday morning and Lynn came in and said, 'Hey, we gotta sign this Garth Brooks. I saw him Saturday night at the showcase; the crowd went absolutely crazy.' And I said, 'Well get him right in here,' and I think Bob Doyle was there that afternoon. And we agreed on a deal."

The next step, Foglesong recalled, was the search for just the right person to produce Garth's sessions.

"Garth had two or three people that he was interested in producing him and we had some suggestions, one of whom was Alan Reynolds, and so the process would be that we would consider all these people and we would look at Garth's suggestions and then we wanted him to sit down with Alan and a couple of other people and get a feel for them, look for compatibility and competence . . . he met with Alan and I don't think he met with the other people at all; he [Garth] was so taken with him. Obviously it was a great choice. It wasn't that long after that they were able to agree on material.

"We released the first single from the album, a song called 'I'm Much Too Young To Feel This Damn Old.' It was not an easy single; we lost the bullet, as we say in the trades, twice. Our company did a great job. We retrieved the bullet and ended up getting a top ten single out of it. It was pretty perilous but I'm very proud of what the company did.

"We had originally planned to release as a second single a song that Moe Bandy later released called 'Nobody Gets Off In This Town.' Garth had a wonderful cut on it. . . . We all felt that the song, 'If Tomorrow Never Comes,' was the big clincher if we could set it up because it was a beautiful ballad, and we ended up doing so well on the first single that we decided to go right for the jugular on 'If Tomorrow Never Comes.' We went in and did a video which turned out to be an outstanding video, a lot of [air] play, a number one video. And Garth['s record sales] really kicked in. We also met with Buddy Lee Agency and agreed to give Garth tour support to get him out [on the road] to work with other acts and subsidize the shortfall that he might be getting because. . . new artists aren't always able to demand enough money [from promoters] to even pay their expenses, much less make any money.

"He did so well so early that we didn't get close [to our budget limit on tour support]. We did have to lend him some money just to pay up his bills here so that he could go out on tour. That seems so strange today because that was only 1989 when all this happened and here it is 1992 and the man is putting a $400,000 addition onto his house and doing so well it's just unbelievable what's happened.

''When we released] the third single, 'Not Counting You,' it was very obvious that we were gonna have at least a gold album. We felt that in the first album there were at least five strong singles. The other song that we were all particularly interested in was a song called 'The Dance,' a Tony Arata song, a classic as we all can say now, but this was a very offbeat song, and this was definitely a song that had to be set up.

''I don't think that you could release a song like

'The Dance' on a brand new artist and get airplay . . . but with 'If Tomorrow Never Comes' as a number one record followed by 'Not Counting You,' which was also a number one record, an up-tempo thing, it was perfect; by that time I had left Capitol, but fortunately the new regime, which was quite outspoken about the fact that they felt that 'Not Counting You' was the last single in the album and they were gonna have to get in and cut another album—fortunately they reconsidered, and released 'The Dance.' 'The Dance,' and the video they did, and they did a great job of marketing and promoting, that's when he just exploded.''

Foglesong had the opportunity to spend some time with Garth as he watched his early career build.

"My instincts told me just in the little audition in my office . . . it was so unusual in that setting I mean he just looked me in the eye as if I were an audience of a thousand people and entertained me. There was something more. I liked his voice a lot. It's really strange . . . there's more voice there than I hear on the recordings; now, I'm not criticizing anybody because obviously what they're doing is right . . . He understood the lyrics. There was a little subtle thing you pick up from somebody who's an actor. I had not seen him do a showcase or perform in front of an audience, but I didn't have to after seeing what he did just for me and our little group of three or four people in the office that day.

"Garth is a fine fellow. At that time he was doing janitorial work in his church. I think he was getting paid for that to help pay his bills; he was having a tough time financially. His mother had been an artist on Capitol... There was a real sentimentality toward Capitol; they wanted to be on Capitol even though Bob Doyle was pitching him to everybody including the people that came and followed me at Capitol, who had turned him down at another label. Everybody in town turned him down. I didn't realize that he was being pitched; the way my conversation with Bob was he was just getting a few opinions but he told me later that, you know, those people had turned him down along with everybody else in town.''

What Bob Doyle was doing had to be done. When you're pitching an artist you can't tell a record executive that your act has been rejected at the other labels or you risk undermining the confidence that executive might otherwise have in your act.

"Garth was very cooperative, a very soft spoken young man who endeared himself to all the staff. He would come in and make phone calls, use our copy machine, he was over at the [Capitol] office a lot, doing interviews, anything we wanted him to do; he was very bright, very clean, and I mean that in all senses of the word, you know, very respectful of people, and his managers [Bob Doyle and Pam Lewis], to my knowledge neither had ever managed before, so they were new in the business and that caused a certain amount of anxiety.

"A little addendum to this is that Clint Black's first product was released around the same time as Garth. Well, Clint exploded right from the word go. His first single was a giant... and there was some [concern] there and [they were saying] we need to do what they're doing for Clint and all that, and, of course, that's really hard to tell. I think we did a great job of getting Garth off the ground... There was some real anxiety because they're looking over and seeing what Clint Black is doing and we're losing our bullet... a lot of anxious moments, some fairly hysteric phone calls and faxes going back and forth... but everybody learned a lot from it. This is the way our business goes; it's of course a pressurized business and everybody *is* looking at what everybody else is doing and everybody's listening to what's happening on the street.''

Foglesong is saying here that when the first single was stuttering its way up the charts, instead of being ecstatic, Garth's management was afraid the label was dropping the ball. By that time everybody in the country music business was aware that a hot, young country artist could sell millions if everything worked out right. It looked like Clint Black was going to be the guy to sell the millions, instead of Garth.

Doyle and Lewis had a right to be worried. Capitol Records in Nashville had had a long history of nonselling artists. One could even speculate that in spite of Garth's sentimental attachment to the label, Capitol had been far from their first choice. Of course, one might be wrong about that too.

''Garth, as an individual, has a lot of integrity,'' continued Foglesong. ''You just say how can anybody be that mature and be so young?... 'If Tomorrow Never Comes'... you know you don't see a person twenty-five or twenty-six years old even thinking about that type of thing. You see somebody in their forties and up writing a lyric like that... That's a heavy, profound song.

''He has a tremendous amount of respect for songwriters, and other people's material. I don't think Garth is going to get caught up into the thing where he has to write every song [on his album]. He hasn't done that. He does write; he's a fine writer and he hooks up with great cowriters but at the same time he's [always looking for great songs from other writers].

''As for his associates, producer Alan Reynolds and comanagers Doyle and Lewis. . . I don't see the greed factor setting in the way you know we all have seen many, many times with artists. And Garth is tremendously loyal and appreciative of the people that spend their money for tickets. He's always going to want to do a good show; I'm sure that his show is going to continue to change and now he already has two tractor

trailers, trucks that are carrying sound and lights, along with his two or three buses. The overhead is tremendous; he's making the big bucks but he's also spending a lot of money and, you know we do get to the point where this is a business. The record business, show business—business is a very important part of it and like any business, in order to make money, you have to spend money. Many acts in the past have been guilty of taking it in but refusing to change their shows, upgrade their band, upgrade the sound and lights and all these things, and they pay the consequences.... Careers don't seem to last as long as they used to and I can't predict, but I think that he is going to do everything he possibly can to produce quality. He's a good guy. He's concerned about people.''

Good guy. Those two words keep popping up when people talk about Garth Brooks. But country music stars are supposed to be good guys. Country music fans *like* good guys. Country artists who ''get above their raisin' '' risk instant rejection from their fans. Over the years fans have made their displeasure perfectly clear even to old favorites like Eddy Arnold or Ray Price when they appeared to abandon their country roots.

We live in an era very different from that which spawned the quasi-pop periods of Arnold and Price. Garth Brooks is selling a million albums a month without having a single on the pop charts. Until recently, if you wanted to hear Garth Brooks on the radio, you had to tune in a country station. Recently, though, other formats have begun to play Garth and other country artists. But at this time, the country in-

dustry doesn't care all that much whether other radio formats play country music. Country music today is insanely happy with itself. Oh, country performers, such as the major hot country hunks, would be pleased as could be if everybody in America would start buying their records, but not one would change his music in the hope of attracting more listeners, the way so many tried to do fifteen years back.

Garth sets the tone. In 1989 he was nothing in the business. Today, without a doubt, he is the most powerful individual in the country music business. He has probably sold more records in the past eighteen months than any record label's entire country *division* ever sold in a similar period. They say that a rising tide lifts all boats. The year the album from *Saturday Night Fever* sold so many millions of records the entire record industry had an extraordinary year because, the experts said, people would walk into a record store to buy *Saturday Night Fever* and then, once inside, make an impulse buy or two. Surely Garth must have a similar effect on country record buyers. So any country music executive, even if he works for a rival record company, prays that Garth Brooks records will continue to sell like Coca-Cola.

Garth grew up in Yukon, Oklahoma, a small town just outside of Oklahoma City, which is smack dab in the middle of the state. At the time Garth was born, Yukon's population was only a couple of thousand, but like many small towns that have turned into suburbs, Yukon has grown substantially since then.

He was born Troyal Garth Brooks, on February 7, 1962, the son of Troyal Raymond and Colleen Carroll Brooks. His father had one child from a previous marriage and his mother had three. Together they had two children, Garth and his sister Kelly. His mother explained how Garth came to be named.

"I had five boys and a girl, didn't get to name any of them but when he came along I said this one I'm gonna name, so I named him after his father and grandfather, Troyal and Garth; his great-great-grandfather was a Confederate general and his name was Garth Ruben Hedges, and I think Garth is one of the strongest names I ever heard."

Garth's father made a decent living as an engineer for Unocal. Garth's mother's musical career was pretty well over by the time Garth was born. In high

Garth Brooks with his parents and wife Sandy.

school, Garth was a three-sport competitor and played in a local band, which meant that he was hot stuff with the girls, and, he says, he took what he could get. In *People Weekly* he described himself to Jim Jerome as follows: "[I] had to be the center of attention. Went from one girl to another. I was pretty shallow."

On stage Garth knows exactly what he is, an entertainer who will do what it takes to get an audience excited, whether it means swinging from a rope, busting up a guitar, or smiling slyly at the sweeties. But in his real life he seems determined to be offstage.

Yet there is something reassuring about a man so

honest that he refuses to put up a front for the media. Part of show business convention is for publicists to plant stories in the media that depict their star clients as being kind, generous, charitable, flawlessly moral, and able to leap tall buildings in a single bound. Garth seems to reject that sort of image building. He told Rick Mitchell of *Request* magazine, "Let's face it, heartthrob is not in the vocabulary for an artist like me. I could understand if I looked in the mirror and saw a man that was handsome and well-built. I see that in George [Strait], Clint [Black] and Alan [Jackson]. When I look in the mirror, I still see the same bum I always did."

At a press conference, one reporter asked him a question about his wardrobe of shirts with wide vertical stripes. This is how he responded.

"When I first took my album [photo] I was 222–223 pounds so I needed the stripes to go down (to look less hefty). I'm right around 195 now and it just hits me that everything I've got is stripes. . . . When my wife does laundry everyone thinks an inmate lives over at our house cause it's just stripes up and down the line outside."

But are we overdoing the "fat old reprobate" thing? In the Rick Mitchell article we read about Garth thrilling a crowd of females at the Woodlands Pavilion in Houston. A woman hands Garth a long-stemmed rose, apparently tells him she loves him, and Garth apparently tells her he loves her too.

"The woman's companion leans over to his buddy and mutters, 'I don't get it. Hell, he's just an old, fat, bald cowboy.' " Then there's that piece in *Forbes* magazine in which "Brooks has been described as having a face like 'a thumb with a hat on it.' "

In today's entertainment world, and today's American demographic, thirty is actually on the young side. Fat isn't a particularly fair description. He's more stocky and muscular with a tendency, like other ex-jocks, to pad up when he doesn't watch himself. His hairline may not be quite what it once was, but there isn't all that much chrome showing; it's always covered by his hat. That brings us to the "thumb with a hat on it" comment, cruel, clever and funny, but not true. Thumbs have no personality. This guy's face is so expressive and full of personality that just watching it makes you smile. (Okay, his hat size is seven and five-eighths, according to *People*, which is a fairly large hat size). So what?

Many media people outside the country music world seem put off or threatened by Garth's success. Maybe it's just that critics feel the professional need to be critical. Whatever the reason, Edna Gundersen of *USA Today* felt moved to lower the boom on Garth one day and Ed Morris, Nashville's resident knight in shining armor, was moved to reply.

Edna had decided that, "If some sense of taste and daring is to be restored to mainstream pop, this hip hillbilly's reign must end." Ed Morris's passionate reply so well underscores the problem country faces in dealing with the pop media that Ed is worth quoting.

"Most rock critics have never grasped the essence of country music. Consequently, they have tended to appreciate only those elements in the music that are least 'country.' Record labels could make a fortune

if they hired such critics in their A & R depart-
ments—and then signed only the acts [the rock crit-
ics] hated.

"Gundersen professes horror that Brooks towers
over such of his betters as Michael Jackson and Guns
'N Roses and grouches that he 'hardly deserves the
unprecedented prominence and glory thrust upon
him.' The subtext of her message, of course, is that
rock is an art form intrinsically superior to country—
but that if country is going to insist on ignoring this
reality, it should at least have the decency to do it
through someone besides Brooks. Gundersen laments
that 'worthier [country-oriented] talents like Jimmie
Dale Gilmore, Lyle Lovett, and Steve Earle' must toil
in Brooks' shadow, ignoring the fact that all three of
these singers have had the same opportunity to en-
chant the public that Brooks did—and have failed to
do so. But what can you expect from rube record buyers, right?"

If you've ever had the desire to be a big star, you
might reflect on the fact that every media bigot with
an ax to grind about country music saves his or her
snidest swipes for Garth Brooks, since Garth right
now is country's most identifiable star and has had
the audacity to woo followers from normally pop age
groups. And the longer Garth, and country, remain
hot, the crueler the media swipes are likely to become.
Fortunately, Mr. Brooks is apparently made of pretty
tough stuff.

In talking about his influences, Garth says that early
in his life he loved George Jones and Merle Haggard,
and later in the seventies got excited about rock
groups like Journey and Kansas. Instead of going to

Garth's fans: his "Friends in Low Places"

school at nearby University of Oklahoma, he opted
for Oklahoma State, where he later picked up a track
scholarship. Just before he got there, he heard George
Strait's recording of "Unwound." That record steered
Garth back to his country roots, and when we get to
the chapter on Strait it might be good to remember
that George's popularity, first established before
Brooks officially stepped onto the beautiful campus
of OSU, grew greater during the seven years that
Brooks was what he called "a George wannabe and
imitator." It is still growing even as his onetime imitator changes the face of country music forever.

One of the more repeated Garth stories relates how
he met his wife.

"How'd I meet her? Oh, you don't wanna know
this, believe me.

"A lot of people take this wrong but Sandy's very much a lady...and I met her as a bouncer in a club and I had to throw her out of the club."

Great. Poor Sandy. Someday when their grandchildren are looking through their celebrated grandpa's aging yellowed clippings, again and again they'll read about the night their gentle and dignified grandmother had a disagreement with someone in the ladies' room of the club and put her fist through a wall. Yes sir, them bars in Oklahoma are *tough*, even in the ladies' room.

They were soon dating, and Garth was positively daffy over her. But he heard the call of Nashville and he had to go. Apparently it wasn't Garth that Nashville was calling the first time around. Although he had come to settle down in Music City and carve out a music career, very shortly he was pulling out of town on the same road that brought him in.

"Why?" You may ask, if you see your favorite entertainers in heroic proportions. Probably he was just not used to being alone. As he told "*US*", "At school, I had my brother. When he graduated, I'd met Sandy, who took care of me. When I came to Nashville it was just me. I just realized that I ain't s— alone. By myself, I'm just a loser."

There's Garth again, honest and vulnerable and so much like the rest of us. Very much like the rest of us. Not always completely honest, says Michael McCall in his biography of Garth.

In 1989, Garth had an interview with a South Bend, Indiana, newspaper, during which he told the reporter that Notre Dame had once offered him a partial football scholarship. There is no evidence, McCall indicates, that such an offer ever occurred.

McCall suggests that when Garth downplays his talents and his character in his comments to the press, he's not being completely truthful about the way he feels about himself. Maybe. His stage behavior certainly points to an individual who is confident about his talent, his world, and his way of doing things. But then, most people go through life with varying levels of self-esteem.

Of Brooks's high school days, McCall writes, "Garth entered a local talent contest . . . singing a country song." We all remember how terribly dictatorial peer conformity in high school could be, and how until very recently it was totally uncool for a high school student to demonstrate any form of appreciation of country music.

"His fellow students," continues McCall, "hooted and laughed before he finished, then razzed him afterward for his choice. He never sang a country song in front of his classmates again—at least not for another decade."

But that doesn't mean he wasn't thinking about country music. Apparently a music career was always on his mind as one of life's alternatives, even though he was a marketing and advertising major at OSU. Again and again when you listen to music business people, you will hear them talk about how smart Garth Brooks is, and how acute is his awareness and understanding of the music business. He spent considerable time in college performing in night spots around the OSU campus. In 1984 he auditioned for Opryland. They offered him a job singing at the theme park but his father demanded that Garth first earn his degree. Initially Garth resisted, but his dad insisted and Garth gave in.

For many years his personal musical idols had been James Taylor and Dan Fogelberg. But by the mid-eighties it had become obvious to many that their genre of music was no longer welcome on contemporary radio. In fact, to someone like Garth, who loved lyrics and melodies, it was becoming clear that country was the only hit format that still provided a home for traditional song-based music.

Garth was also reading about the coming of the new traditionalists in country music. He may have felt that as the old stars faded, and the young ones moved in, there might be a place for him. Of such stuff, dreams are made.

Warner Brothers record executive Nick Hunter talks about Garth:

"When this is all said and done, when the big hillbilly splash dies down, or the artists that are big now go to the happy CD pile in the sky, if you look back, I think Randy Travis will be remembered as the one that brought traditional country back, and I think Garth Brooks will be remembered—of course as the big act—but I think that his best known trait will be that he upgraded country artists' shows by leaps and bounds. Unless the guy is just a spellbinding singer, the stand-there, not-movin', singin' is not gonna be as readily acceptable over a long period of time [as it once was] . . . you're gonna have to give the people some entertainment value for their dollar too . . . and I think [Garth] will show this industry that if you put on a great show and get everybody talking, what it does to record sales and your whole career.''

Sometime around the American advent of the Beatles it became a sign of artistic purity for recording artists to write their own songs. The concept is, of course, pure hogwash. The idea is to record the best songs available. But pop fans considered that their idols were delivering pieces of their deepest soul in the songs they composed themselves. It never occurred to these fans that in many cases their idols were just looking for a way to get another hit. There's nothing necessarily wrong with that. After all, making hit records was the way they made their living.

For many years, the country music community held the last highly concentrated group of people who made their living writing songs for artists who were looking for a hit song to record. It was in some ways a great system because these writers, who worked twelve months a year writing songs and never left their legal pads behind to spend a couple of months out on the road, became extremely proficient at their craft and wrote many wonderful songs. But the system had some flaws, too. Because these writers had to go through layers of publishers, A & R people, and producers before their songs could make it to an artist, their songs often lacked the adventurous quality that sends music in new, creative directions. The idea was to write a song that had balance—the excitement to turn people on, without the kind of controversial lines that make nervous, bureaucratic label employees shut off the tape recorder.

Then came Randy Travis and the rest. By that time

country fans were beginning to catch on to the idea of ''the singer as songwriter.'' Record labels that used to fear singer/songwriters as potential egomaniacs who might shut their minds to good outside songs now encouraged their young artists to write. The idea was that these artists would know who they were and would work hard to write songs that reinforced the images they were attempting to project.

That idea has worked pretty well with most of the young hunks, but it has worked *perfectly* with Garth Brooks. Garth has cowritten some fantastic songs for his albums, and yet, three of his biggest singles, ''The Dance,'' ''Friends In Low Places,'' and ''Two Of A

Kind (Workin' On A Full House)'' were *not* written by Garth.

That's the kind of musical integrity that was not understood by the pop fans of the sixties who used to criticize Three Dog Night because they recorded other people's songs. Garth Brooks, his producer Alan Reynolds, and his manager Bob Doyle all have long experience listening for great songs. Each of them can recognize one when he hears it.

They also appreciate the people who write great songs. That's how Garth started writing with Kim Williams, an East Tennessean who was unknown on Music Row until the past few years. During this time he has written or cowritten "If The Devil Danced In Empty Pockets" for Joe Diffie, five songs recorded by Doug Stone, three by George Strait, and one by George Jones, in addition to numerous cuts by less celebrated artists.

Oh yes, and three recorded by Garth Brooks and released in those multi-multi-platinum albums that make fortunes for virtually everybody involved in their creation. Included among those three was "Papa Loved Mama," from Garth's third album, *Ropin' The Wind*. The song originated with the following quatrain:

> *Papa loved mama*
> *Mama loved men*
> *Mama's in the graveyard*
> *Papa's in the pen.*

"Originally," said Kim, "we thought that it was a Carl Sandburg [verse]. It was attributed to him in this book I had called *I Wish I'd a Said that*. . . .I'd found this thing and I told Garth about it. I said, Carl Sandburg said this and Garth said, 'Well, what'll we do if we write that thing?'

"I said, 'Well I don't know, we'll split it with Carl Sandburg, I guess.' I said I don't mind writin' something with Carl Sandburg and he can't complain. We just kinda had a joke about it but we had a ball writin' the song . . . I was living in a little apartment off of Edge Hill [a street in Nashville near Music Row], a little roach palace. Man, I'd sprayed it; the roaches were everywhere. I'd swept those up before Garth came over, but I can remember when we decided that the means of doin' mama in gonna be a truck driver runnin' a truck through there; it was a real fun thing and I think they captured the fun in the tracks when they cut it too.

"After he cut it and they got serious about it . . . you know, Garth's a real meticulous person; he's not gonna do anything unless he feels like it's right. So then he said they're gonna have to find out for sure where it [the quatrain] came from . . . they started researching it but they couldn't find anything in Carl Sandburg's 'literary files,' I guess you would say, that had anything about it so they got more and more worried. If it wasn't Sandburg's, whose was it? They finally talked to Carl Sandburg's daughter and [she told them] it's an excerpt from an old folk song that he used to do around the campfire."

Very old songs become part of the public domain. Anybody can use them any way they want, so Kim Williams and Garth Brooks had clear title to what eventually became a very successful song for Garth.

"I've heard some people talk about the violence in the song but to me it's like a cartoon; you don't really take the violence serious," Williams remarked.

Williams first met Garth when Kim was writing for a small music publishing company. A songplugger from another company heard some of Kim's songs and pitched them to Garth.

"This was before Garth's first album came out," Kim recalled. "Garth loved the wordplay in one song in particular, a song called "Right To Remain Silent," a song later recorded by Doug Stone. "Garth told the songplugger, 'I'd like to write with this guy.' And of course [at that time] nobody knew who Garth Brooks was. He *did* have a deal with Capitol but his first album wasn't even out. It was my first shot to write with anybody who was on a label. It was a big thing for me but (laughs) turned out to be a heckuva lot bigger thing than anybody ever imagined. It's real odd lookin' back, but since then I've written with several major writers—and I won't call any names—that Bob Doyle had asked to go write with Garth that hadn't done it. And boy they are sick."

To understand how sick those writers are you can figure that Kim Williams's three Garth Brooks cuts are worth hundreds of thousands of dollars to him. He has also cowritten a dozen other songs with Garth and will probably write more with him. Some of them will probably be recorded by Mr. Brooks. Now, remember that Kim Williams has had considerable success with songs recorded by other major country artists. Nevertheless, it is those Garth Brooks cuts that may make a wealthy man out of the East Tennessean who was

well into his thirties before he really committed himself to a songwriting career.

"I just feel lucky that I even got the shot to start with. We just hit it off. I mean, we went to lunch, he

and I and this plugger [songplugger] the first day and
then we started scheduling writing sessions.''

Garth Brooks. The fastest selling artist in the history of country music. Probably the most important
person to happen to country since Hank Williams, Sr.
Outside of his musical talents, what kind of personality traits have helped him to put so much distance
between himself and his hot hunky contemporaries?
Kim Williams sat across the table from a young man
who was still months away from his first hit. What
was his first impression of Garth?

''Real likable. And I think as I got to know him
better, I know the word is used and abused, but it's
the only word I know of, he's charismatic.''

That instant likability he felt when he first sat
across the table from Garth, is that what Garth carries
onto the stage with him? Is it that charisma that gets
'em stompin' and cheering all night long? Kim's answer was surprising.

''No,'' he responded, flatly. ''There's two different
people to me. When he's on stage he's got energy.
When you're writing with him he's such a laid back
person. I mean, he gets excited like everybody else
when you're writin' something good but. . . The stage
presence I saw in the last two three shows [that I've
attended], he's developed gradually, just got better
and better and better. I think he's worked hard on it,
just like he worked hard on his songwriting. He's a
different character out on stage; he goes out just to
really entertain.''

When two songwriters collaborate they generally
bring different gifts with them to the table. In the old
Tin Pan Alley days the songs almost always differ-

entiated between the composer and the lyricist. One was a musician. The other was a poet. Today the songwriting credits usually read, "words and music by Joe Blow and Mary Blach." Each puts in a little here and a little there. Nevertheless, one is stronger at this, the other is more gifted at that. What about Garth?

"I think he's great melodically," said Williams, "but he's also got a knack for knowing what the song should say. My strength is playing with lines, bouncing words back and forth but he, on the other hand, while you're throwing out these lines, is trying to make sure the song is structured and saying exactly what it needs to say. And why I love to write with him is, he loves writin' little slices of life. And they're not always pretty. And they're not always happy, although some of them are. To be honest with you, when we wrote 'Papa Loved Mama' I didn't have any idea that he would cut that. I don't know if he did. We just had a ball writin' it.

"The day that we finished 'Papa Loved Mama' he came out to my house because it got so crazy you couldn't write around his office or this office or any of the other ones; he's just so popular and so big, and . . . we kinda hugged, I feel real close to Garth and hadn't seen him in awhile; he'd been out on the road and I said, 'Well, man, how's it feel, you're on top of the mountain.' He's already at four million, maybe five million on 'No Fences' and was getting ready to cut 'Ropin' The Wind' . . . and he looked tired that day and he said, 'I like what I got, but I love what I had.' I said, 'Boy, that sounds like a song.' I've never had a chance to really ask him about it again, but I took it that he really does miss this writing, this chance just to get up everyday and come in and talk awhile, and then maybe write. That's the way I always write and that's the way he writes. You might talk for two hours and then decide, 'Hey, you remember that idea we talked about,' and then you start writing. More of a real loose, fun thing. I know that Garth is enjoying his success, but I know, at times, you miss a lot of the simpler things, because you're being pushed from one thing to another, or thrown, or pulled, not that Garth's being pushed, he's his own motivator, but he's got a lot of things to do now. You know along with his success there comes more and more responsibility.

"I remember we'd take turns buying breakfast on the days we would write and I could remember Garth coming in and I'd say, 'Well it's my time to buy breakfast, where are we eatin'?' And he said, 'naw I'm not eatin' today, man. I don't want to eat any breakfast today. I've got a photo session in two weeks and if I don't slow down, they're gonna have to take an aerial photo.' "

The music business can be a jealous business, and Kim knows of a few artists, or what he characterizes as "would-be artists," who can't understand Garth's success. But, he adds, quickly, "most of the artists that I've written with—and I write with quite a few artists now—are grateful because they realize he's extending their boundaries too, especially to the young people. Garth is one of the first ones to start drawin' in these real young kids, ten, eleven, twelve years old. I'm forty-four years old and I felt like an old man at one of his concerts. But on the other hand there *is* a good wide range of people who come out to see him.''

Kim pauses for a moment, and looks around the room at all the expensive audio equipment that helps him create some of country music's best songs.

''You know, he was rollin' pretty good. He had three number ones off his first album, and he had cut his second album. I know by the way this town thinks that he got some advice against puttin' out 'Friends In Low Places.' I'm sure that there was some people said, 'I don't know about this song. This is a drinkin' song, Garth. But...' That's where Garth's different. [He thinks] 'Does this feel right? Is this something that I ought to do?' And he makes that judgment and he goes with it. Knowin' all the time, and he talks about it all the time, walkin' this line. You're on the edge. I think he does the same thing when he's bein' interviewed out in public. He *knows* there's a chance in what he's doin'.

''I can tell you something else. He's gone through this whole thing from when I'd say, 'I'm writin' with Garth Brooks, he's a new artist on Capitol' [and they'd say] 'GARTH! What kinda name's Garth? Garth who?' He's gone from that, in a couple of years to being, you know, a legend, and I think he's enjoyed that. I think his head has been in the clouds, but his feet's been on the ground... and that takes a pretty big man.''

One of the problems Garth will have to face is the American tradition of building up our show business heroes and then tearing them down. Recently I was talking to a Nashville music veteran, a successful songwriter and publisher. He had seen one of Garth's shows, and he was shaking his head as he described the performance.

"All that jumpin' around, that exaggerated 'wrowwwrrr.' " He made that growling sound that has become a Garth Brooks trademark. He went on to admit that the kids at the show loved it and that he loved most of Garth's music, but he wondered just how long Garth could continue at his present popularity plateau with that kind of stage persona.

He had a point. A minor point. Kids are fickle about their taste in artists. There's no reason to believe that a year from now America's twelve-year-olds will care about the music of Garth Brooks.

But so what? If his album sales diminish from seven million copies per album to one or two million faithful Garth Brooks collectors, then where's the problem? Garth Brooks will probably change his show to suit the tastes of his fans, while continuing to record the best music he can find or write. He will slow down some, write more, and probably have a little more time to smell the honeysuckle. The only fly in the ointment will be the national press. They'll write pieces about the decline of Garth Brooks, and if there aren't a few hot risers fighting for his spot as king of the mountain, they'll write pieces about the death of country music.

Any doubts about the future security of Garth's throne were muted in September of '92 when Liberty released his new album, *The Chase*, and his Christmas album, *Beyond The Season*. The albums immediately dashed to slots one and two on the Billboard pop album chart. When he and his wife had their new baby, pictures of the Brookses enjoying familial bliss suddenly sprouted all over the national media like dandelions after a spring rain.

There can be no question that Garth Brooks is the hottest recording artist in the history of country music, and one of the hottest in the history of American pop music. Period.

5

Alan Jackson

OF ALL THE COUNTRY HUNKS, ALAN JACKSON may be the most underrated.

Garth, of course, is in a class by himself. Clint Black got off to a fast start on the charts and his marriage into the world of Hollywood has only increased his media coverage. Randy Travis and George Strait have been so successful for so long that they may be the youngest living legends country music has ever known. Travis Tritt's image is so distinct from the rest that you can't help but notice.

Not that nobody notices Alan Jackson. You look at this man and you don't forget him. But his first album, *Here In The Real World*, was released only three years ago in the shadow of the early record sales battles between Garth Brooks and Clint Black. In that short, short time, here is what Alan Jackson has done.

Four consecutive number one singles came off the first album, including at least two country classics, "Here In The Real World" and "Chasin' That Neon Rainbow." The album went gold within five months and platinum within a year. The follow-up album, *Don't Rock The Jukebox*, was released in May of 1991 and reached gold status in just two months. It too has soared far beyond the platinum sales level, and has spawned a couple of number one singles, "Dallas," and the title cut, which may be his most popular single yet. The two albums have combined sales of over three million units.

Has the business taken notice of him? You bet they have. Over the past two years he has been nominated by almost every award-giving body in nearly every appropriate country category. He's also taken home his share of the hardware.

In 1991 *Radio & Records* chose Alan Best New Artist Of The Year. TNN/*Music City News* Awards selected him as their Star Of Tomorrow and his debut album, *Here In The Real World*, as the Album Of The Year. The Academy Of Country Music, the West Coast's most prestigious country music organization, made him their Top New Male Artist Of The Year. The 1991 *Music City News* Country Songwriters Awards awarded him Song of the Year ("Here In The Real World"). And in 1992 his album *Don't Rock The Jukebox* was chosen as Favorite Country Album by the American Music Awards.

He's made the required national TV appearances, appeared on numerous national magazine covers, and plays to packed houses. Alan Jackson has arrived. All blond-haired, blue-eyed, six-foot-four of him, topped by that perfect hundred dollar white Stetson hat.

An early article on Alan by *People* tells us that Alan Eugene Jackson "grew up in Newnan, Georgia, in a house his granddad converted from a tool shed.

Alan Jackson—first FanFair

He slept in a hallway until he was ten and the oldest of his four sisters moved out.''

While he was attending South Georgia College he was working day jobs and playing clubs on the weekends. Alan was not considering a music career as a legitimate alternative. His wife Denise, however, understood where his real dreams lay. She was a flight attendant and they meet many people. One day she met Glen Campbell in an Atlanta airport and told Glen about her husband. Glen gave her his business card. *People* describes this encounter as Alan's ''big break,'' and that's why you should never believe what you read about show business in the big magazines.

Margie McGraw in *Spec's Rhythm & Views* says that before this encounter, Denise was out of town, in training as a flight attendant for USAir. With some time on his hands, Alan drove to Nashville, like many a hopeful, just to see what he could see. He must have done a lot more than gawk around Music Row because the Nashville Network offered him a job working in their mail room. Two weeks later, Alan and Denise relocated to Nashville.

Within a year he did have a writing gig with Glen Campbell, but that doesn't qualify as a big break either. Plenty of songwriters get writing deals with publishing companies and then a year later they're on the bus going back to wherever they came from.

In most real show business stories, the term big break just doesn't apply. Case in point: Alan Jackson. According to veteran country journalist Bob Allen in *Country Music* magazine, Jackson was ''turned down flat at least once (in some cases more than once) by

every major label when he first started making the
rounds in Nashville back in the mid-1980s. Jackson
can even laugh the last laugh now about the major-
label A & R person who advised him to seek another
profession. The label rep kissed Jackson off with the
assurance that he simply didn't have 'star potential.' ''

Ah, now that's more like it. Alan Jackson did not
become a star because Denise bumped into Glen
Campbell in an airport in Atlanta although you
might say she started the ball rolling. Alan Jackson
became a star because he kept the dream alive after
everybody turned him down. The fact is, most artists who become stars get told sometime during
their careers that they don't have the talent, or the
right style, or the right look, to be a star. As the
great film scriptwriter/author William Goldman has
repeatedly written, ''Nobody Knows Anything'' and
people like Alan Jackson instinctively seem to understand that. So when the inevitable rejections
come, they may get discouraged for awhile, but they
don't stay down for long.

Alan Jackson's big break came when Clive Davis
decided to establish a country branch of his successful
Arista label in Nashville, and chose the talented Tim
Dubois to run it. In Alan's music, Tim heard what
others before him had missed—either that, or Alan
was a better singer and songwriter than he had been
earlier in his career.

Even though the record labels have promoted
their hunks as great singer/songwriters, these new
stars still rely heavily on the Nashville songwriting
community to write hits for them. Alan Jackson is

one hunk who has earned an enormous amount of respect within the songwriting community for the quality of his songs. He has cowritten many of his biggest hits, and some of his best work has been cowritten with Alabama-bred Jim McBride. Jim has had a view from the catbird's seat throughout most of Alan's early career.

"About four years ago," says Jim, "I was a staff writer down at EMI [a powerful, worldwide music publishing organization]. I had seen Alan in the office a time or two, and we hadn't been introduced, but I saw this big tall guy who wore a cowboy hat and I thought, gosh, he looks like a country music star and I wondered if he's any good; I wondered if he could sing."

By that time McBride had obtained a pretty fair reputation as a songwriter.

"I believe Alan called me one day and asked if I would write with him and I said, sure, so we got together and he played me a song that he had written that ultimately ended up on his first album, called *Home*. And it was about his life growing up, about his family; and I played him a song called 'Dixie Boy,' that I had written about *my* life growin' up, and Alabama had recorded *it* on the *Closer You Get* album, and I think from those two songs we realized that we were coming from, basically, the very same place. The kind of music, straight ahead country music, that he loved and I did too. I think we decided that we'd probably work together real well.

"We started talkin' about Hank Williams' music and George Jones and Gene Watson and Vern Gosden and he very much liked Randy Travis. He's got a pure country heart. He sings from the heart and writes from the heart and I appreciated that.

"This was at least a year before he had his first hit. The first song we wrote was 'Chasin' That Neon Rainbow.' I'd had that idea for two years in a notebook and I didn't know what to do with it. I knew what it was about but I had never played clubs or anything. At the time I met Alan he had this old Dodge van and he would tell me how he'd drive . . . to Florida and he'd be playing three, four sets a night [in some little club] and there wouldn't hardly be anybody there. And nobody knew who he was. And then he'd go to Arkansas and do the same thing. And I said, 'You're tellin' me what this idea's about.' I'd never known how to write it and so we basically just told his story, what he was goin' through at the time."

When songwriters come up with a good song they generally get very impatient to pitch that song to the first important name artist scheduled to record that the song fits. But Alan Jackson, like so many of the hunks who have "made it," was focused on becoming a hit recording artist, so his perspective was different.

"He told me the first time we got together and started writing that he was trying to get a record deal and he asked me at that time if I would be willing to hold on to any songs we wrote together until such time as he got a record deal. And after hearing him sing the one song that he sang me, I said, 'Sure.' I believed in him so much from the very first day. I was totally convinced that he was gonna be a big star. I said, 'Sure, anything we write, I'll talk to my publisher and let's hold these things for you.' And that's what we did. We didn't pitch any of the songs and then, when he got ready to record, we ended up with three of them on the first album.''

Jim McBride had made a wise investment of time and talent in Alan Jackson. His *Here In The Real World* album has made Jim McBride a healthy pile of cash, but we have to remember that when McBride started writing with Alan, Alan was just one of dozens and dozens of country artists in Nashville, chasing that neon rainbow, struggling to get a record deal and hoping that if they do, some big hits will come out of it.

Jim McBride has found a marvelous cowriter in Alan Jackson, and the results of this collaboration have been impressive.

''We've written twelve songs together,'' says McBride. ''He's cut six of them, George Jones cut one, and Randy Travis cut one, and some independent artist cut another.'' Nine songs recorded out of twelve written. That's an almost unheard of success rate. Many successful writers count themselves fortunate if one out of every four songs they write gets recorded.

''We wrote one song and oddly enough Alan cut it and they thought it sounded a little George Straitish so he played it for Randy Travis and it's on Randy's *High Lonesome* album.''

Why was the song good for George Strait or Randy Travis but not good for Alan Jackson? McBride pointed out that it was a western swing song, the kind of song that is so identified with George Strait that it was considered unsuitable for Alan Jackson, even though Jackson cowrote it.

"It's almost like that [kind of song] belongs to George," McBride says. "And if you cut a swing song, you're trying to be like George so they wanted to get around that, and Randy's voice sounded different enough that it didn't sound [like a George Strait record] at all."

Many songwriters in Nashville take a wry view of artists who, they believe, pass themselves off as songwriters while writing on the coattails of their cowriters who are "the real writers." Some of this is jealousy, and some of it may have a bit of truth. Alan Jackson has the reputation, among many Nashville songwriters, of *being* a "real songwriter." McBride talked about Alan Jackson's songwriting gifts.

"As I said before, Alan writes from the heart, so therefore, I feel like he appeals to the common everyday person out there. And he says things a little differently. They may not be exactly grammatically correct—and I do the same thing sometimes—and I've learned to trust Alan's instincts. If he feels good about a line or a word, I didn't know it at the time, but now I know that it worked. It's just him. He's being honest and coming from the heart, and I don't think you can go wrong. He is indeed a *real* songwriter. I've had people ask me this question before. Right when I first met him, he played me two or three songs he had written by himself that ended up on the first album. I thought they were great. They're still some of my favorite songs."

Songwriting partners often open up their emotions to each other. McBride was writing with Jackson during those early days when there was no certainty that Alan was *ever* going to get a recording deal.

"He was anxious to get a record deal and get out there and I would say [to him], 'You know, I know some people who have been here longer than you that it hasn't happened for them yet.' And I don't think that helped him a whole lot. He was ready for it to happen. And there were a couple of times when it looked like something was going to happen at a particular label and it fell through [really disappointing him], but we've talked about it since and things happen for a reason. He's exactly where he should be. Clive Davis and Tim Dubois and Arista came along, and he was their first artist."

It's terribly unusual for a new record label in Nashville to click with a platinum-selling artist right away. Songwriters are, and always have been, absolutely essential to Nashville's Music Row. Yet many people in Nashville's recording industry are ignorant about the role of songwriters, nor do they respect the people who write the songs that are the basis of all those music business jobs. So McBride smiles when he thinks about Tim DuBois, the man most responsible for Arista's unparalleled early success.

"Somebody made the comment," he says, "said look what happened when a songwriter started running a record label. I thought that was an interesting observation."

Returning to the subject of his favorite cowriter, McBride recalled that "He *knew* what he wanted to do. That's one of the things I admired about Alan. It wasn't like, well let's find a [musical] direction or something. He's like Randy Travis. What you see and what you hear is exactly what he is. He would get a little down [when a record deal would fall through] but there was always something out there, another possibility out there on the horizon."

Since Jackson knew exactly what kind of music he wanted to do, there must have been times, during country's "countrypolitan" phase, when he wondered just where he could fit in.

"He was kind of like me and a lot of other people [during that time] thinking, 'Where is the real country music?' for a few years there, and he was very much encouraged when he started hearing Randy Travis. He thought, well, maybe there's hope. The fact that Randy made it encouraged Alan. I think he felt like maybe Randy opened the door, that maybe he could go through. He thought, 'if they will accept Randy, maybe there'll be a place for me too.' "

Once Arista became interested in Alan, McBride recalls, it didn't take very long for them to sign him.

"I remember seeing Tim Dubois at a showcase that Alan did at Douglas Corner and I told Tim that 'This guy is gonna be a star.' I said, 'I felt that way one other time and it was Randy Travis back in '82.'

"Besides the fact that Alan's a great singer and the way he looked, the songs that Alan did were very much a part of it. And once Tim saw him and heard him, as I recall, it wasn't a real long time before the deal was done.

"I think any reservations Alan had about Arista being a pop label coming to town were offset by the fact that he was their first project and was gonna get the attention."

After the years of hoping and working and waiting, you can imagine how Jackson felt about his first major record deal.

"He was very much ready to go. He was ready to get on the bus [the rented or owned tour bus artists and their bands ride all over the country from show to show]. In the studio and on the bus. 'I'm finally gonna get my shot. I'm finally gonna do it and we'll see what happens!' "

Jackson's first single was "Blue-Blooded Woman," but it was the second release, "Here In The Real World," that launched the Alan Jackson phenomenon.

"Oh, yeah. It just took off. And I remember he'd called me after 'Here In The Real World' came out. He'd go out and play somewhere. And the reaction of the fans . . . was kind of scary at first and, he couldn't believe it. He'd call me and say, 'Man, we had all these people at the show, and they were just kinda goin' nuts, they were grabbin' at me'—all that shocked him. He couldn't believe all that was going on.

"He's not in it for the quick kill or for the short run. He would like to have a career like Strait or, you know you talk about Conway Twitty or somebody. And nobody stays on top forever. I remember when Johnny Cash was the hottest thing in the world."

Now that may seem obvious to a fan. Anybody would rather have a career that lasts twenty years than one that lasts five. But what McBride is saying is that Alan Jackson enjoys the entertainment profession, and that if five years down the road his record sales were down and he was playing the dinner clubs instead of the twenty thousand seat superstar venues, then he'd still be on the road entertaining people because that's what he set out to do from the beginning and that's what he is. This is especially poignant when you consider that Alan Jackson, like many of his fellow hunks, will make enough money over the next few years to live in squirelike retirement for the rest of his life if he so chooses.

But as Jim McBride said, Alan Jackson knows what he wants to do.

Has success changed Alan Jackson?

"Not personalitywise. He's just much, much busier. That happens to all artists when they get hot. I don't think Randy Travis has changed. Randy to me is just like the day I met him. He's just got a lot more money.

"There are more demands on their time. Alan has very little time of his own."

Too little time to hang out with his old buddy and cowriter Jim McBride? At the time of this interview, they hadn't written together for months. But I ran into McBride a week or two later and he told me they had just written together in the interim.

"I went out on the road with him a couple of weeks ago and we wrote three things. We worked some on the bus but usually we'd start like 9:30 or 10:00 [in the morning] at the hotel and write until time to go to the building [the auditorium] and it worked out real good. I mean we worked hard. We'd continue to write in between sound checks, you know, and then the next morning we'd wake up wherever we were gonna be [and continue working on the song where we'd left off before the show the night before]. He's probably one of the easiest writers, if not the easiest writer, I've ever had to work with. It's fun; it's not like work at all."

It's difficult to understand the kind of dedication that motivates an artist like Alan Jackson. Road travel is wearying and boring. It makes you want to pass the time doing mindless things when you're not actually involved with the show. Many a country star has lost his way on the road over the years, to booze and drugs, and women, and other unimaginable forms of degenerate behavior. It's a measure of just how much Alan Jackson loves what he's doing that he can spend time in his dressing room between sound checks struggling with his cowriter to come up with a line for a song that may or may not ever get recorded. One of the hallmarks of Alan Jackson and many of

his fellow hunks is that success is so new to them that it still feels fresh and fun. And it shows on their albums and in their performances.

It's interesting to note the impression he has made on some of the more knowledgeable media people in the country music industry. David Ross of *Music Row* magazine calls Alan Jackson's songwriting sensational. "And as a result," he says, "his music has really clicked with the fans because he's got something to say in almost every record they released."

His Arista bio has a little gem of an anecdote

about a guest appearance on "Hee Haw." Apparently, during the taping, he found himself thinking, "Boy, here I am on 'Hee Haw,' in the middle of the cornfield. I guess I really have made it." I'll bet he'd make a good neighbor to have just down the road.

6

Travis Tritt

A T THIS TIME IN COUNTRY MUSIC, WHEN THE three letter word with the wide brim is still the universal topping for country hunks, it's sort of interesting that one of the very hottest wears a motorcycle helmet. His explanation, through *People* magazine:

"No one should wear a cowboy hat unless he feels comfortable sitting on a horse. I'm more comfortable on a Harley."

But like most of the other hunks, Travis Tritt is not trying to make a cosmic statement. He rides a Harley because he likes to ride a motorcycle, not because he is projecting a kick-your-butt, I-hate-the-establishment image.

People outside the South often do not understand the close relationship between country music and rock 'n roll. Northerners are so aware of the segregation that went on for so long in the South that they ignore the enormous amount of cultural sharing that occurred between the races over the years. That sharing was especially apparent in southern music. Southern churches, black and white, knew the joy of gospel rhythms, and along the Mississippi River southern whites heard the blues. Many of the old country stars, from Hank Williams to Bill Monroe, learned from black musicians. And when a portion of rhythm and blues was renamed rock 'n roll and passed on to white audiences, it was Sun Records in Memphis that gave us early authentic white rock 'n roll singers like Carl Perkins, Johnny Cash, and Elvis.

I say authentic because they didn't have to make a calculated decision to choose this music; they were simply doing the music that they'd been hearing and liking for some time. The engineer of many of those old Sun sessions, who also wrote some of their best known songs, was Jack Clement, known in Nashville as "Cowboy," a longtime musical iconoclast who

Travis Tritt

once stated, in all seriousness, that "bluegrass was the father of rock 'n roll."

The reason I bring this all up is to help us to understand the music of Travis Tritt. Is Travis a country singer? Is he a rock 'n roller? The answer to both questions is yes. Travis Tritt does the music that he likes to do, and he happens to be fortunate that he's come along at a time when country radio, records, and fans are ready to appreciate quality, no matter what genre label is applied to it.

His first album, *Country Club*, went platinum. His second album, *It's All About To Change*, went double platinum in the summer of 1992. If there is a country candidate likely to break through to the Garth plateau, Travis Tritt could be the one. In a recent media release, Tritt described his musical mission as follows:

"We're trying to break down the barriers between different kinds of music. I'm a firm believer that there's only two kinds of music: good and bad. I like to describe my music as a triangle. On one side is a folk influence from people like James Taylor, Larry Gatlin, and John Denver. On the second side is George Jones and Merle Haggard: that type of music. And then on the third side is the Allman Brothers and the Marshall Tucker Band. They're all balanced together, all a part of what I do."

Interesting. A musical mix not all that different from that of Garth Brooks. Both Brooks and Tritt (and numerous other country hunks) look to James Taylor as well as Jones and Haggard for inspiration. Maybe Garth has a little more Taylor and Haggard, a little less Allman Brothers in his mix, but they're all present in his music.

* * *

Promotion whiz Nick Hunter who now works for Giant Records was at Warner Brothers when Travis got started there, and from his point of view, here is how Travis Tritt got from here to there in no time at all:

"Danny Davenport, who is the local Warner Brothers promotion man in Atlanta . . . called me, and he said, 'I've been working with a guy about two years, we've cut an album on a little bitty label and we've put it out somewhat, and I want you to come and see the guy.' Well he sent me the record first and I listened and I, really, didn't like it very much . . . it just wasn't very good. So, [they] started working with him some more, and I went down to see him [live on stage] and I said, 'Hey, this guy's really good,' so I came back to Jim Ed [Norman, president of Warner Brothers' Nashville division] and I said, 'Jim Ed, any time we've ever asked Danny to help us try and cross a record over or do something extra on a Hank, Jr., project . . . Davenport has been there for us.' And I said, 'This kid isn't that bad by any stretch of the imagination. Why don't we give him a shot?' So Jim Ed sent Doug Grau down to listen to him and Doug came back with glowing reports and then we signed him. Then, when the record ["Country Club"] was cut but it wasn't out yet . . . Danny called me up and he said, 'I want one of two managers to manage him, either Ken Kragen or Chuck Morris.' "

I might interject here that Chuck Morris is a successful manager best known for his handling of Highway 101, while Ken Kragen is the California-based gentleman who is credited with so much of Kenny Rogers's incredible run of crossover success during the late seventies and eighties.

"...I said, 'Kragen will tell me that he no longer wants to manage people, he now calls up chairmans of boards and, won't be interested but I'm gonna call him anyway,' so I called Kragen and said, 'I found this guy,' and he quickly went into his 'I don't do that anymore bla-bla-bla and I'm really out of that business now except for Kenny Rogers...' and I said, 'Well, this guy is really good, let me send you a tape,' [expecting him to want nothing to do with it] and a week or two goes by and I call Kragen and I said, 'Oh by the way, did you get the tape?' and he said, 'Uh, yeah, in fact, Travis and Danny are gonna be here at three o'clock this afternoon'—this was in L.A.—'I'm flying him out, the guy is great, everybody who heard the tape is just jumping up and down and I'm real interested in doing this thing.'

"They've been real good for each other because Ken, with his history and his connections, can open a lot of doors that many managers cannot...and Travis is a smart guy, he works hard, I mean, he'll do the radio stuff [visit radio stations] do the in-stores [visit record stores], he meets people, I mean he's just a real, real good guy.

"And every once in a while he'll, like all of them do, you know, get a little bent out of shape but Davenport gets a two-by-four out and slaps him side of the head and he's fine."

With a rocker like Tritt, why did Warner Brothers choose such an obviously country song like "Country Club" to introduce him to his public? Nick, one of

Nashville's shrewdest music business heads, talked about the changing rock scene.

"When you sit down and look at the market-place anymore, there's no market out there for new guitar rock 'n roll. I mean it really doesn't exist. As an example Bob Brown, who manages Huey Lewis and the News; he's an old acquaintance of mine and he came by to see me one day when Huey was in town doing the Reba McEntire video that he was in...I said to him, 'Man, isn't it gettin' tough out there, with Huey and your basic guitar rock 'n roll?' He kind of laughed and he says, 'Funny you'd say guitar rock 'n roll; when we picked our first or second single off the album whatever it was, we submitted it [to the record company] and they asked us to go in, take the guitar off and put a synthesizer on there to make it a little more palatable to CHR [Contemporary Hit Radio].'

"When you go back to Travis Tritt, there really isn't much of a market out there for that, and he's a *great* country singer...and his biggest hits, with the exception of 'Here's A Quarter (Call Someone Who Cares)' and 'Country Club' have all been what I guess you'd call power ballads. He throws in a semi-rock thing or two on his albums and in his show he'll look and see who's there and if it's a younger crowd, he'll crank it up and if it isn't, he won't.

"The other thing is, you're still seeing a lot of artists come along who have come to this town as song-writers and who are not prepared to go out and hit that road and make that sacrifice."

What he is referring to is that at the beginning of an artist's career, to get his name and face before the people, record companies will send him out on the road for weeks at a time, playing small clubs or as an opening act, often making little money, with high overhead. The record company may provide funds for tour support but that money doesn't come free; it's usually charged against the artist's royalties. The result is that the artist spends a great deal of energy and sometimes goes deeply into debt at the beginning of his recording career, hoping that it will all be worth it in the long run. Songwriters who have been making good money sitting in their cozy offices and writing hits are especially reluctant to travel around the country in an old uncomfortable bus. They're generally not hungry enough to make the sacrifices that a brand new artist is willing to make.

"Oh, Tritt loves it," says Nick Hunter. "All Travis needed was someone to get him a bus and show him where to go. As soon as he got that, he was off and running."

Just how much bigger will Travis Tritt get?

Nick Hunter thinks carefully before he answers. It's part of the unreal nature of country music today that you can talk about a young artist whose album has sold more than a million and a half units and seriously ask a question like that.

"We'll probably be about a million-seven when this single is finished and then, over a period of time, with the release of the next [single] we'll do another three hundred thousand, so this will be a double platinum album." (Since this interview was completed, Travis has indeed gone double platinum).

"When the perception is that your second album is bigger than your first you see careers in higher gears than you do with artists whose second album wasn't as big as the first, or wasn't perceived as big as the first one. And the three who stand out in my mind as really kickin' it in gear the second [album] were of course Garth, and then Randy, and now Travis."

What Nick is talking about, of course, is careers that start fast and then build even higher rather than those artists whose uniqueness only lasts as long as that exciting first album and then winds down into mediocrity.

"You know, I think that one of the major differences between now and the Urban Cowboy, when we took country music and kind of made it pop music, this is *country* music, and I think there is no way to tell at all what artists connect and what artists don't connect. Jimmy Bowen had a great line, he said, 'Randy Travis could sing off key on TV and sell one hundred thousand albums the next day.' Whatever it is in that one artist really gets to the public and the public relates to him, that something in their music that gets people out of their house to go into their K-Mart, Wal-Mart, Tower and go buy a record, while you have all these guys who are selling all these records, there are just as many guys sittin' there and some of them even making better records, that you couldn't get people out of their house to go buy their record if you tossed it in the front yard and said, here, walk out and get it, it's free!

"I do have a fear though. I remember one time somebody called me and asked me how long did I think this thing could go on and I said, 'As long as people [in the country music industry] keep looking for different and unique stuff and don't try to clone Randy Travis twenty-five times.'

"... We're getting stale," he says, "but we have come up with some who are different. And I think that those are the ones who are gonna stand out above the rest. Just recently when I was down in Florida I literally drove across the state from Sarasota over to West Palm Beach...and you can find a zillion country stations...and there were a lot of people on the radio that—all sound alike. I think it's gonna end up being a problem for us somewhere down the line— now of course, the music business has always done that. There was Elvis and Eddie Cochrane and Gene Vincent and Conway...."

"The real test on these people [who sound like Randy] is listen to the brand new record for the first time and tell me who it is. We need to continue to grow and look for new and different things and I know that's an easy thing to say and a hard thing to do."

Nick has spent many hours with Travis Tritt. He has gotten to know him and care about him personally, and root for him.

"I'll tell you what. He loves his free time. He's not a big athlete. He'll do a little fishing. He's just a good guy ... there's a little redneck in him in there, you know, bein' from Georgia and what have you. I still like one of his best lines 'cause, when I first met him, he'd been divorced twice and I said, 'Are you gettin' ready to get married again?' and he says, 'No, every two years I'm gonna buy a woman that I don't like a new house.' "

Travis Tritt knew he wanted to be a singer when

he was four years old, and he never gave up the dream, though occasionally he soft-pedaled it.

"I always knew I wanted to do it [sing] but I was sort of stressed about it because my family really wasn't behind it. They had good reasons for it," he told Lisa Smith during their interview session for the *Gavin Report*.

"They didn't want me to end up like Elvis. When I was a kid it seemed like everything you read about people in the music business was bad."

But he loved it, and knew he could do it, so he went after it, and his family hated it. At the age of eighteen he married for the first time. By that time he was pleasing everybody except himself by working "a real job" in the heating and air-conditioning business. A year later his marriage broke up, leaving him free to be as irresponsible as he pleased. His parents were not happy.

And they weren't that impressed when Travis signed his record deal with Warner Brothers. They'd heard a great deal about the record business and just about all of it was pure poison.

So he signed with Warner Brothers and his folks kept the light burning in the front room. Warner Brothers released "Country Club" and the light stayed on. According to Travis, they didn't decide that they could save on candle money until the record went top ten. Travis Tritt was born to wise parents.

In the old pre-rock 'n roll days, major record labels gave certain gifted men the title of "head of artists and repertoire," (A & R) or some such title. These individuals signed artists to record for their label, and then found songs for them. Then they hired an arranger and the musicians, set up a recording session, and created a record. Some of these A & R men, most notably Mitch Miller, attained legendary status.

In Nashville today all major record labels have an A & R department. The employees of that department do a job fairly similar to what those old A & R men did, taking into account how much the art of making records has changed. Today many of these A & R people are women. It is interesting to note that while women have entered many power positions in the once male sanctuaries of the Nashville music business, few of them have made the transition from A & R person to producer, the individual who actually supervises recording sessions. That will change.

One of Nashville's best young A & R men is Doug Grau, A & R Director at Warner Brothers Records. Five years after coming to Warner Brothers to work in their mail room, Doug had his first major A & R project, overseeing the recording career of an unknown Georgian named Travis Tritt. Doug must have done something right, and he is apparently doing something right with Little Texas, the new, hot group, he co-produces at Warner Brothers.

In the course of his involvement with Travis he has learned a lot about this man who is carving a platinum niche for hot country music with the southern rock accent.

''I had moved from promotion to A & R in January of '88 and had been just gettin' my feet wet, kinda getting used to what my job was gonna be. I was actually in the studio with the Marcy Brothers [a Warner Brothers recording act]—I had stopped by to say, 'Hi,' and see how things were going. I got a call from Nick [Hunter] and he said, 'Well, I'm here with Danny Davenport and he's got this artist that I'd like you to hear. Can you come right now?' I said, 'Sure, I'll be right there.'

"Now Danny primarily promotes rock radio stations, gets Madonna and The Talking Heads and all that thing played on the radio for Warner Brothers. But Danny had always had a home studio and was always dabbling with music."

Danny played the sides Nick Hunter alluded to earlier and told Doug that he'd been working with this performer for two and a half years.

"What I felt about the album was that Travis was at that point already a great singer and that it was just a matter of finding him the right kind of songs. Early on they did a little bit of everything as they were trying to decide what he was about as an artist. There was a song where he would sound like Steve Wariner, then there was a song where he'd sound like Willie Nelson. He didn't really have his own defined sound so I mentioned to Danny that I'd like to go see him perform.

"We went on down to Atlanta and had dinner with the whole band. It was a real family consciousness thing. Travis already had a full-scale band and had been playing with them for about six months, playing club dates around Atlanta. Before that he'd worked as a duo and he'd done a single act for years, so he had been playing in the market, I don't know, four, five, six years, before I got there in '88.

"After dinner we went to Travis's house, went down to his basement and did a little rehearsal, and the band played for me, and confirmed that this guy was a great singer but I felt that we didn't really have our finger on what we needed as a sound. I made several trips to Atlanta because Travis was always playin'. He played at a club called Murph's for about six months. It was a little hole-in-the-wall biker bar but he played there Thursday, Friday, and Saturday night and was able to work on new songs.

"What I wanted to do with Travis was to bring in a producer that really would give me a lot of time and help develop a sound around this guy 'cause I said, 'Man, I've got a great singer, but I'm really not sure what he's about and what's gonna be his mark, cause he's been playing club gigs for so long, he does everybody', I mean, part of [being a club singer is] you're a human jukebox, you know? And when you're up there you're doing Willie Nelson, and you're doing Waylon Jennings, and you're doing Ray Charles. He used to do a great act where he did 'Seven Spanish Angels' and he would sing Willie's part then he would sing Ray's part, did 'em both to a tee. He'd have the headband for Willie then he'd put on the sunglasses and do Ray's part.

"We had just hired a staff producer named Greg Brown and the only thing Greg had done to that point was a couple of sides on a new artist named Chris Austin [who, as a member of Reba McEntire's band, was later killed in a plane crash].

"One of the big reasons Greg came to Nashville was he loved Waylon Jennings, especially Waylon's early stuff. That was one of the common threads that

I noticed with Travis, and so I began to talk to Travis: 'What if we worked with Greg Brown?' Travis at first was saying, 'Greg Brown! Who's that? I wanna work with Barry Beckett [producer of Hank Williams, Jr., and other big country acts].' There was even a movement in Travis's organization to get Hank Williams, Jr., to produce Travis Tritt.

"I told Travis that what we really need is somebody who's gonna take the time and mold a sound around you because you're a great singer and we need to have the package together." By that, Doug meant that mysterious combination of songs, producer, and artist that brings out the musical uniqueness of that particular artist.

"So we began to work with Greg and Greg would make these trips to Atlanta with me. We would go once or twice a month, go see a couple of [Travis's] shows, hang out, listen to songs. We used to have a pitch sheet that we'd mail around town [telling publishers and writers for which artists Warner Brothers was looking for songs] and his name was on there forever, it seemed like, and people were constantly asking, 'You ever gonna record stuff on this guy? Hey! What's the deal?'

Music publishers even found Travis' name confusing. "For awhile we didn't even put his name [on the pitch sheet] because people were saying things like, 'Well, you're gonna have to change his name, 'cause there's Randy Travis, and what do you mean by Tritt? What kind of name is that? I've never heard of anything like that. I mean, what's a Tritt?'

"Everybody said that was a given, that we were gonna have to change his name, so we developed notepads full of names, from James Gunn, to Travis Wayne, we went as James Travis Tritt for awhile— we tried a bunch of different things. Nothing felt right. It didn't feel honest, you know.

"Finally we got ready for our first session. Originally we'd been approaching Travis as a development deal [a deal in which the label cuts some sessions on the artist with the understanding that if and when they record a song or two that knock their socks off, then they'll sign the artist to a *real* deal]. But one night I ran into Jim Ed [Jim Ed Norman, head of Warner Brothers Nashville] and Jim Ed said, 'What are you working on?'

"I said we're workin' on Travis Tritt. He said, 'Ah, I've heard some good things about him. Well where are you?'

"I said we're gettin' ready to go in and cut some demos and see what we got.

"He said, 'Well, what do you think?'

"And I said, 'This guy's really good, I think we're gonna have something here.'

"He says, 'Well, then go ahead and sign him to the label, because I really think that you guys have got a good team, and everything is goin' together real well.' So we made it official before we went into the studio and we went in to cut records. And on the initial session we cut 'Country Club,' which is a song Mike Sebastian, who was with New Clarion Music, had brought to us and, actually, Alan Jackson was singin' the demo. We cut a song Travis had written with Larry Alderman called 'Son Of The New South,' we cut a song called 'Sign Of The Times' that Travis had written by himself, a song called 'Help Me Hold On,' that Travis wrote with Pat Terry, and then we also cut a song called 'The Road Home,' that Steward Harris and Jim McBride had written.

"The obvious first single was 'Country Club' just based on the novel aspects of it. We almost talked ourselves out of 'Country Club' because it was so obvious or so novel. The person who was the big champion for 'Country Club' was Travis. He really felt it was a great first single."

Here is a good place to explain that in country music for many years record executives reserved the right to choose single releases for their artists and only the most powerful artists were able to exercise control over the records they made and released. Today many of the record labels make it a point to involve even brand new artists in the selection of songs for recording and release.

"That's an approach that Jim Ed has used ever since he's been with the company. He says we really want to take the artist into consideration. Historically, the artist has been run over in the music business from time to time. So Jim Ed has always said, 'Well, theirs [the artists'] is gonna be the final decision.' We'll advise them and hope that they're right. Really, we try to make these decisions together, but when it comes down to where we can't come to a conclusion that's obvious, it comes down to the artist or somebody in that camp having to say, well, this'll be the first single.

"We still were concerned that the mixes weren't quite right, so we delayed the release of the single and had Scott Hendricks, who is a well known engineer in town, do the remixes on the first five songs.

"All this is happening the first part of 1989. The delay is goin' on and Travis was going through a period where he was frustrated with the system. . . . He was beginning to say, 'Hey, I'm ready to get goin', what's the holdup? What's goin' on?' And I'm having to preach patience.

" 'I'm ready to play,' he's saying. 'I've been playing Atlanta long enough.' He had started stretching out to book some regional clubs; he had started working in Ocala, Florida, Augusta, Georgia."

At this point he's anxious for people to hear his music.

"Oh, yeah. There's nothin' like playing your single [live, onstage] and people know it, know the words. That's always a great first experience for any artist. I think he felt that it was partially my lack of experience that was causing him to be so slow to move through the system."

"Move through the system." A funny way to describe putting a record out, but very accurate. The country music record business has become very much big business, with big money on the line. It's a business so competitive that no one wants to put that first record out until everything is as right as it can be. The delays continued through the spring and Tritt must have been ready to throw a fit.

"Finally we schedule a record and it's scheduled for July! There's a lot of concern then because a group we had called Billy Hill had their first single coming out about the same time. And Nick felt that they would be real competitive against each other, both being "southern" in nature [as in tending toward southern rock]. And so we held onto the Tritt record and delayed it for like a month and a half.''

Then Doug and Tritt's acting manager talked Jim Ed Norman into letting them do a video on Travis, but when the video was made and turned in, the company didn't like it. Not the proper image. And then Travis and his acting manager weren't able to work out a proper management contract. That's when California industry heavyweight Ken Kragen got involved.

''Part of the way Nick approached it with Ken was, 'Do you wanna manage our next platinum artist?' And Ken said, 'Well, sure I do, who wouldn't. Send me a tape.' At that point Ken was able to be a help with me in getting the video released because I felt that there was something in that video that showed a lighter side of Travis that would help break him, and Ken saw the same thing, so we were able to release the video and the single. The video really helped expose that first single. CMT viewers really reacted to Travis and they took that video to number one, and 'Country Club' the single went to, I wanna say, number nine, initially. The success of 'Country Club' allowed us to get our album ready for release.''

They released five singles off that first album, which built sales to about seven hundred fifty thousand, then when the second album got hot, the first album earned platinum status of a million plus, now approaching a million and a half units.

Most of today's hot country hunks are active songwriters. Their labels encourage their songwriting, a departure from the way it used to be in country music.

"[From the beginning] I wanted Travis to be involved in the creation of the songs as a songwriter. On his independent album, I had heard flashes of brilliance. There'd be a great hookline. There'd be some great imagery in a verse, but the structure was too long-winded. The songs were all four and a half minutes long.

"So Greg and I sat down and made a wish list of possible co-writers for Travis. Stewart Harris, Jim McBride, Don Schlitz [writer or co-writer of 'The Gambler,' and other country classics]. Greg came up with Larry Alderman because Larry is a real 'southern guy'; just a very long list that we made up and we began to set up some writing visits for Travis and he would come up through the summer. He'd drive his old Ford pickup to town and I'd put him up at the Hall of Fame or Shoney's [two motels near Music Row], and he'd do some writing for three or four days, then he'd go back to Atlanta and play during the weekend.

"Some of the songs that came out of those sessions were 'Son Of The New South' from the first album, that he wrote with Larry Alderman, 'Drift Off To Dream' that he wrote with Stuart Harris. I just wanted him to be involved in the writing. I thought, there's another chance for him to be unique and outstanding, and have a leg up on not sounding like everybody else."

But that didn't mean that the door was closed to outside writers, by any means.

"Out of the hits that we had, 'Country Club,' he didn't write. 'I'm Gonna Be Somebody,' he did not write. He did not write, 'The Whiskey Ain't Workin'.'

Marty Stuart and Ronnie Scaife wrote that one. So three out of the nine singles he's had out so far, he didn't write. But, some of his biggest, including, 'Here's A Quarter,' which is almost an anthem, he wrote by himself.'' As a writer, Travis Tritt has come a long way in a short time from the independent album with the great hooklines and the four and a half minute lyrics.

Doug is very proud of the quality of Travis's albums, and he believes that the level of competition is so great that it demands high quality.

''The whole level of making albums in Nashville [has improved substantially] maybe since about '86 [since] Randy Travis's *Storms Of Life*. I mean there's a great album, my personal opinion. From top to bottom, I mean every song is on there for a reason, and that kind of thing really changed Nashville. Used to be our albums were you had two hit singles and just a bunch of garbage. You listen to those albums and nobody wants to. You buy the singles because who wants to hear that other garbage, you know?''

Like Nick Hunter, Doug Grau has become very fond of Travis Tritt. Travis is the cornerstone of Doug's A & R career. Before him, Doug was the new kid on the block, listening to hundreds of songs a week, looking for hits for Warner Brothers artists. Travis gave Doug his big chance to oversee a recording artist's career from the beginning, searching for a sound, developing his image, reassuring him along the road, ''through the system'' as Doug would put it.

''Travis works real hard. His favorite thing to do is play music. He's a performer from the word go. I mean, he would have carried on without me, or War-

ner Brothers, or Nick Hunter or Danny Davenport or anybody. In the early days before the 'Country Club' record came out, he would book these regional dates. He'd have his pickup, put a trailer on the back of it, and a couple of the guys in the band would drive it to wherever they needed to go. His charge out of this thing is playing live.

"He would book the dates—in the early days he was his own booking agent—he would do the business, he'd take care of the money, he'd make sure the band was paid, he'd worry about the P.A. gear. That was part of what put a lot of pressure on me. He, the artist, was going through the frustrations of wantin' to have a single out so he could book dates for bigger dollars, and I'd have to say, 'Now, bear with me here, it's gonna pay off in the end. Trust me.' After some of the success we've had we can kinda look back upon that and say, 'Well, you know, it's panned out pretty good.' "

When your first album in the big time goes platinum plus it would seem that you'd qualify as an overnight success. But some successes are less overnight than others.

"We began on the project in March of 1988. The album actually came out in March of 1990. So there were two years in the making of Travis being an overnight success. Prior to that he had worked for upwards of six years himself. Then he worked with Danny for another three, so, by the time 'Country Club' became a hit he was ready. He played everywhere! Through the help of Brian Williams at Third National Bank— put a plug in for my friend—they were able to get him a bus and get him on the road. Travis played every hole in the wall that he could. The guy went crazy. Played his heart out."

Now a little tale about the very beginning of the story of Travis and Doug.

"Initially, Danny was pitching the act to me as a group, Travis Tritt and True Grit. He said, 'The band is what's special here, I want you to sign the band.' But after seeing them a couple of times, I said, 'The big star is Travis. We gotta focus on him. That's the only thing I'm interested in signing.' Most of the band members are still the same. And they're friends of mine. Some of the charm of going to see Travis is the little band that he's got. It's a little kick-butt band. They've got their chops together and they play well together. But Travis is the star.

"I said to him once, 'You know you really ought to get on an exercise program. You know, build up or something, a little bit, because Randy Travis does it.'

"He said, 'Look, I get my exercise on stage. I sweat for two hours when I play. But that's all. I don't mow the grass. I don't wanna play tennis, I don't wanna run, I don't wanna do anything else.' Last year was an unbelievable year. He played almost 250 dates, I think. This year he's scaled back to about 150 and probably will continue that kind of a pace for the rest of his career 'cause he's a working artist.''

Would he like to be a movie star?

"He would like to be. In the 'Anymore' video I think he did really well. He acted out a role; he was Mac Singleton, a veteran who had lost the use of his legs, and they're actually talking about the possibility of making that into a TV movie. They're pitching the idea around. It might happen. When we read the concept [of the video] I said, 'Aw, man, Travis, I don't know, this is really asking for you to do a lot of stuff.' We decided, well, if it doesn't come out right we just won't put the video out, but it came out real well.

"He's taken up a few hobbies. He likes to go fishing. He's gettin' a new house on a lake maybe an hour north of Marietta. Really likes riding his Harley Davidson motorcycle. . . he's taken up [scuba] diving.

"But the general spirit of Travis Tritt is, he wants to play. He's ready to go. Always."

In 1991 Travis found a high energy musical soul mate in Marty Stuart. According to Nashville's best known country music journalist, Robert K. Oermann,

Tritt and Stuart were waiting backstage at the "Nashville Now" TV show when they started talking about hair.

Now, there is no way you could confuse Travis Tritt's coiffure with that of George Strait or present-day Garth Brooks, and Marty Stuart's locks also tend to flow, by today's standards anyway, though John Anderson makes them all look like they're wearing crewcuts. So these two sometime-rockers were discussing the present trend of "hat acts" and suggesting that they call themselves "hair acts." Having established that particular bond, they became aware of the styles of music that they shared. Both of them had a firm grounding in traditional country music and yet both of them loved to rock 'n roll. The result was their "No Hats Tour," which drew fans like flies to a picnic, and then "The Whiskey Ain't Working," which became a big duet hit for them.

What tells you most about the two of them is the fact that their shared interest so easily turned into a shared tour. Travis Tritt and Marty Stuart had long careers as performers before they became recording artists and they both find their primary expression as artists in playing before live audiences.

The style of their show, like that of Garth's, is grooved for younger audiences. In the Oermann article, Tritt described it as "a pretty spectacular show. It's a high-energy thing, country music with a rock 'n roll attitude.

"If you looked at the set, you'd think Aerosmith or Bon Jovi was playing that night."

Not so very long ago, any "country" artist who

had dared to make that kind of live music would have drawn a tremendous amount of flak from local press reviewers complaining that a rock 'n roller was attempting to pass himself off as country. No doubt some of that still goes on in the boonies, but a substantial number of media people know that even the rockin'est of today's hunks knows his country roots and embraces them. He just refuses to be restricted by them and has the right audience support to prove it. Experienced performers like Travis Tritt, former "human jukeboxes" if you will, can pretty well gauge the mix of their audiences, and adjust their programs to satisfy the folks who attend that night.

I believe that more than any other country artist, with the possible exception of Garth Brooks, Travis Tritt represents the change that has taken place in country music over the past half decade. On one hand, the so-called older fans of country music (aged thirty-five to fifty) have grown up with rock 'n roll and don't mind some basic rock 'n roll in their concerts so long as it's song-oriented and not mind-numbing like music from the late sixties. On the other hand, younger audiences seem to be thrilled with the music mix presented by artists like Travis Tritt, Marty Stuart, and Garth Brooks. For the first time in decades, a popular music is uniting, rather than dividing, the generations.

7

Randy Travis

IMAGINE, IF YOU WILL, COUNTRY MUSIC BEFORE Randy Travis. Oh, I know, Alabama was selling millions of records. George Strait and Ricky Skaggs albums were going gold with very traditional material. And many exciting new acts were coming on the scene. Country radio had finally kicked the Urban Cowboy malaise and country artists were no longer recording elevator music in search of the pop crossover.

But country had no real sense of direction. It was still paying too much attention to whether or not the "other" folks might think these performers were hillbillies.

And then came Randy Travis. It is almost impossible to imagine what Randy Travis has meant to country music. Without Randy Travis there is no Garth Brooks. No Alan Jackson. No Clint Black.

And without Martha Sharp there is no Randy Travis.

Who is Martha Sharp? She's a very special woman. Several decades ago she was a songwriter who wrote

Naomi Judd: "He's so cute."

a couple of major pop hits, including Sandy Posey's "Single Girl."

For a number of years she was a secretary on Nashville's Music Row, usually for Larry Butler, the great producer who launched the second career of Kenny Rogers. In the early eighties Jimmy Bowen chose Martha to work in A & R for him at Warner/Elektra. Martha was soon in a position where she knew she would have to come up with something to justify her existence at the label. She came up with Randy Travis and their story begins back in 1985.

"The story goes back to, I guess, November of 1985. I had been in a CMA [Country Music Association] subcommittee meeting, marketing subcommittee, and they had brought in some people to talk about marketing country music and new ways to increase our market share. Things were really down after the Urban Cowboy phenomenon. There was a retailer there, and one of the things he said really stuck out in my mind. And that was, his customers didn't think that what they were hearing on the radio was country music. I don't remember anything else about the meeting. It was like this light went off in my head. I put that together with the idea that we needed younger demographics and it occurred to me that maybe somebody that was truly country but young and also attractive might have some interest to the people out there who felt that they [were being ignored].

"Because I had known for some time that the Urban Cowboy thing had turned off a lot of people in the fact that there were a lot of artists coming in, trying to be country, to leap on that bandwagon. And I really wanted somebody who didn't want to do anything but just be country. We had a roster full of people who wanted to cross over [to the pop charts] and I wanted somebody who didn't want to cross over, somebody that loved country music. The way that it happened is unbelievable to me when I look back on it.

"I had lunch with Judy Harris [a successful Nashville publishing executive] and I said I'm looking for a young male artist who doesn't want to do anything but country music and she said, 'Randy Ray.'

"And I said, 'Oh yeah, you know, you had played me a demo of a song and he was singing on it and I liked it pretty much, who do I talk to about it?' and so, she told me, Charlie Monk [another publishing veteran] was working with him. That afternoon I ran into Charlie Monk at a function at ASCAP and I said, 'So tell me what's going on with Randy Ray,' and he said, 'Well, I'm doing some demos on him now, I'm trying to get some stuff together for Bowen [who by this time was heading up MCA Records' Nashville operation]. But I'll let you hear it.'

"And I said, 'Yeah, well, why don't you do that.' He brought me a tape and I listened, and I was pretty interested. He said, 'Well, you need to go out and see him at the Palace [Nashville Palace, a club near Opryland where Randy was employed in the kitchen.]'.

"He [Charlie Monk] took me out there for dinner and Randy sang and, I guess, cooked too, that night, and he was just so sweet and so shy, and he sang a song called 'Reasons I Cheat' and I just fell in love with him. But I thought, boy, this is a real scary thing. Nobody at Warner Brothers is going to hear this. And so I was thrashing around, I thought, what am I gonna do, what am I gonna do?"

At this point Kyle Lehning enters the picture. Kyle is a successful producer best known for his work with England Dan and John Ford Coley and Dan Seals.

"Kyle called me and said, 'You know I hear you're looking at [Randy] and I'd like to throw my hat in the ring as producer' and I thought, this is what I need, this will give me leverage because I knew Kyle didn't go after just anybody. I'd offered him acts before that he'd turned down. That was real intriguing to me [how different Randy was from the other acts Kyle had produced]. It was scary to me too. So, I thought, I'm just gonna do it. And I just did it. And I know that people [at Warner Brothers who didn't see eye to eye with Martha] really thought, 'Well, we're rid of her now, you know.' And I spent a lot of sleepless nights. But we were in the studio by January, that's how fast it happened. I don't even know if the contracts were signed. On that first session he cut 'On The Other Hand.'

"We had a record ['On The Other Hand'] out pretty soon after that and it did well in some markets but we couldn't pull it through. I know why but I don't want to talk about it. Yeah, maybe I will talk about it. The truth of the matter is people here didn't take it seriously. There was a response [out there] that was so overwhelming that people here thought it was faked. The fact of the matter is that a radio station called and said, 'We're getting hundreds of calls on this kid Randy Travis. We want to know, who is he?' The lead was not followed up because people were so unprepared for it. This was so against everything that they had been led to believe, which was that we need to get more pop to get the younger demographics. The prevailing opinion was he was too country to make it.

"He'd gone back in the studio and cut '1982' and we put that out and the rest is really history. It was a real exciting time and I remember going down to, I think it was Athens, Georgia, some little place where he played and he and Lib [Randy's manager and now his wife] and I were driving there in a gold Lincoln and you could sense what was happening even then at the beginning, when he was playing little joints with a house band. To stand in the back of the club and hear that voice, it was just phenomenal. But when I really knew, was when I heard it on the radio, first

time. And I credit Kyle with being able to know, to stay out of Randy's way.''

One of the wonders of this story is how Kyle Lehning was able to bridge the differences between pop-style records and fundamental country records. Pop records tend to be layered, with complex arrangements and mixes that have the lead voice blending with the instrument tracks. Basic country records, on the other hand, tend to require spare, simple arrangements with the lead voice far out in front of the instruments, because in country the lyric is so important to the listener. Few in the country music business might have imagined Kyle Lehning cutting country records, but he made the transition to Randy Travis without a hitch. The records sounded great right from the beginning.

''He said, 'I don't like country music but I love to listen to this guy.' And obviously there was something to that because a lot of people that don't like country music learned—hey, truth be told, I learned to like country music from Randy. I mean I've never been a major country music fan. I've always liked music and I've always liked all kinds of music, but . . . a dyed-in-the-wool country fan I wasn't. I'm pretty ignorant really about a lot of country music except for the stuff that went pop and that is the quality in him [that makes country fans out of noncountry fans] and that's why his sales are what they are.''

Record labels sometimes make strange decisions. Occasionally they even make strange decisions that wind up making a lot of sense. Back in the 1970s RCA Records had a very country artist named Gary

Stewart. Like many hard country artists of the time, he was having a terrible time breaking through.

RCA had put out a record on him called "Drinkin' Thing" that was a stone stiff, which is another way of saying that few radio stations played it and fewer fans cared. Six months later, at a staff meeting, producer Roy Dea was asked what he thought RCA should put out for a new release on Gary Stewart. He replied something like, "I think we oughta put out 'Drinkin' Thing' again. We haven't got anything better in the can."

So RCA re-released "Drinkin' Thing," and this time the record made it to top five on the *Billboard* country singles chart.

Now it was time to put out a follow-up single to Randy Travis's career-launching "1982." The Warner Brothers brain trust chose "On The Other Hand," the song that had failed to get Randy's career rolling the first time around.

"I think it might have originally been Kyle's idea [to re-release 'On The Other Hand.']," Martha remembers. "Then a bunch of us talked about it in a sort of abstract kind of way," which is another way of saying that nobody there really had the gall to come right out and suggest it. "And then, I think, Nick decided that we should try to do that." Nick Hunter is one of those people with very strong opinions who is not afraid to back them up with action. Sometimes he's right on and sometimes he's dead wrong, but you know where he stands. In this case his decision was a historic one. "On The Other Hand" is a Randy Travis record we will remember long after most of the others are forgotten.

One of the reasons Martha Sharp may have been nervous about signing Randy was that she knew that many of the people who worked in the Nashville offices didn't like hard country much more than their counterparts in the California office did. Did Randy and his success change the hearts and minds of these crypto-pop people?

"There are still people here who are not traditional country fans. They're Randy fans. Not just because he's done wonderful things for the company but because he's such a delightful human being and because he makes such wonderful music. One of the things that I've been so grateful for in working with Randy was that he has a wonderful ear for songs. And if an artist doesn't have that, then all my work in trying to drag hit songs up and present them to him is useless."

One of Martha Sharp's functions is to find songs that she feels fit Randy Travis. On a typical weekend she'll take home dozens of cassettes presented to her by publishers and writers in and out of Nashville. She will listen to at least a portion of each tape, separating what she considers to be the best from the rest. Then she'll listen to them again and keep the very best to play for Randy and his producer, Kyle Lehning. A & R people get very frustrated when they find a song they feel is a smash, only to have it turned down by the artist. Martha has confidence in Randy's ability to "hear" a great song.

"I hear from people who work with other artists who have great vocal talent but don't have that ear. Randy has that ear, and the people here really respect Randy and they love him as a human being, and, let's face it, he's helped to build this company into what

Randy sings, "I'm gonna love you forever..."
to country legend Minnie Pearl.

it is. But there are a lot of people (at Warner Brothers) who still prefer less traditional kinds of music, and that's cool. Personally I listen to classical music when I listen for enjoyment, which I don't get to do very much. But I love listening to Randy. It took people a long time, not just in this company but on the Row, in the music business in general, to see [Randy] as anything but a fluke. I don't know why they didn't figure it out sooner but it took RCA two years or something to finally get around to signing Clint Black and figuring it out, and then some of the others followed suit. But if they'd looked around [they would have seen that] the only things before Randy that were selling were George Strait and Ricky Skaggs.''

Why did it take a Randy Travis to get the other labels interested in traditional artists? Why didn't George Strait open the eyes of Music Row?

"There are two reasons, I think. One is because George's fan base is basically Texas. He is basically the Second Coming in Texas. It doesn't translate much outside of Texas, a little bit but not very much. He was [only] selling gold at that time. When Randy started selling platinum and double platinum, people started paying attention. And when 'Always And Forever' came out and he became a major star, everybody thought, well maybe we better do something about this. That's the only thing I can assume."

According to Martha, Randy was the one who showed record people that there is a market for traditional country.

"That's not to say anybody just dropped anything else and said okay let's concentrate on traditional country. They didn't do it here [at Warner Brothers] or anywhere else. And probably never will."

It's not uncommon to find a record executive who has fond feelings for an artist so successful that he makes the executive's job feel secure. Martha Sharp's feelings for Randy Travis run much deeper than that, as you may have noticed. To Martha, Randy is a wonder, a grown man whom success has failed to deprive of his innocence and fundamental decency.

"One of the things that always intrigued me about Randy was his attraction for little kids. Especially after 'Diggin' Up Bones' came out. 'Diggin' Up Bones' was their song. They love it! When he would do it in concert and there were kids in the audience, the kids would get up on the parents' shoulders. I remember coming back from Europe, the second time he was over there. Coming back we were in the New York airport. I had to go get a ticket change and I was standing on line and Randy was over sitting down with a bunch of folks. And this guy was standing there with his, oh, eleven-year-old daughter and he said, 'I know you think that's Randy Travis but it's not.' And she said, 'Yeah it is, yes it is...' So finally I turned to them and I [whispered] 'Yes it is,' so she went over and got his autograph and to see him with her—and it's, it's everybody. It's the way he treats people with such respect and interest. People will come up and he will be in the middle of a meal in a funky old restaurant. He'll have his fork halfway up to his mouth, people will want his autograph and he'll just—put his fork down and he'll talk to them about themselves, and ask them what they do and where they're from. I've just never seen anything like it; I'd say, 'Back off, you fool, can't you see I'm busy eatin' lunch?!' You know and he's just so gracious. I *have* seen him sometimes pushed to the wall but, you know he'll say, (imitating him she speaks in a deep voice, slowly, softly) 'Well, that guy makes me kinda lose my temper and I sure don't wanna lose my temper.' He's just amazing. That kind of low-key warmth and graciousness he has is just real special.''

What does Randy Travis mean to country music? Try this on for size. The death of Hank Williams was an even greater disaster for country music than imagined. At the time of Hank Williams, other major country stars were searching out audiences beyond country fans. Consider Eddy Arnold and Tennessee Ernie Ford, for example. But Hank Williams, Sr., was living proof that a country singer could be strictly a country singer and yet claim a wide circle of fans buying millions of records.

When Hank died, that prototype died with him. A scant three years later Elvis's first RCA record, "Heartbreak Hotel," was released, and within a short time no self-respecting adolescent would have been caught dead listening to a country radio format.

Back in the early sixties, when Nashville began rebuilding its shattered musical base, starting with the radio stations, the primary parameters were, keep it country enough to fit rough definitions of the genre, but make it as pop as possible to grab the kids, or if not them, the remnants of middle-class adult record buyers. Thus countrypolitan arrived, with its background string arrangements and positive love songs. The best of this music was much better than the rock critics made it out to be, but it was far too limited to create the excitement that a dynamic popular music should create.

When the so-called outlaw and Urban Cowboy movements broke through to new audiences and new sales records, country record executives thought that they had uncovered a secret. It was really the same tired formula that the founders of Music Row had brewed, with some success: that if you make country pop enough, you'll rope in those disenfranchised audiences who like their music familiar and not too radical.

There were two problems with that idea. One, the major sales are with the kids, and kids want their music to be a fresh departure from last year's music and, two, it's hard to find fresh music among artists who are performing within parameters.

Recall the words of Martha Sharp: "I'm looking for a male artist who doesn't want to do anything but country music." Sounds limiting, doesn't it? Sounds uncreative, doesn't it?

But it's not. Because Randy Travis was only interested in hard country music, and because he knew good country music when he heard it, he didn't have to calculate; he didn't have to operate within stated parameters. Randy did what came natural to him, and because he did it very well, he touched many people, including enough younger people to bring his *Storms Of Life* album to triple platinum in the spring of 1992. Randy Travis had shown America that it was okay to be country. It was fine to be country. It was *great* to be country. As Fred Rose did with Hank, Martha Sharp and Kyle Lehning let Randy's music happen naturally, and never added a track or changed a mix because hey, maybe if we do this, the pop stations will play it.

And all the hunks that followed Randy Travis? Some of them, like Alan Jackson, are just straight country like Randy. Others, like Garth Brooks and Travis Tritt, perform a wider variety of sound. But in one way they all follow Randy's lead: they let their hearts tell them what music they want to make.

Make no mistake about it, this is *the* golden age of country music. How long it will last is, of course, impossible to tell. The same kids who think that a particular singer is wonderful today may think he's yesterday's garbage tomorrow. But this I'll bet: just

as the rock 'n roll music of the fifties and early sixties has become a classic music played by oldies radio stations around the country, someday, many years hence, record repackagers will pick up on the country music of the late eighties and early nineties, and people will buy it because so much of it is so good.

Randy Travis and Martha Sharp were the ones who really started the era rolling.

"When he went out on the road at the beginning, when it first started breaking," Martha remembers, "he was on the road all the time, and he wasn't used to it. And all of a sudden he was, like, the savior of country music. That's a big burden to lay on a cook from the Nashville Palace. So between that and the road schedule that they had at the beginning, he started developing vocal problems, and that bothered him greatly, because he's one of those people who wants to go out and give one hundred percent every show. And when he doesn't feel like he's done well, he just kind of berates himself and feels bad, feels like he hasn't done his job.

"So it was kind of a bad time, but at the same time he took the steps to take care of it and went to a vocal coach who taught him how to warm up. He had mixed emotions, and he never verbalized this to me. He was . . . otherwise real relaxed about it.

"There was always this sense of destiny about him that, he knew that he was gonna make it—I don't know that he ever had any sense that he was gonna make it like this. But I never felt he was astounded by it, or impressed by it, or any of these things. I've seen artists change overnight and Randy didn't change. I *did* see him gain confidence and become much more a man of the world; he was exposed to new things. He'd been pretty sheltered. As he got out there in the world, he just sort of became a sponge and he soaked things up and he was always open to new experiences and new foods, when he was traveling around the world. So I saw him gain in confidence but I've never seen him become what I've seen a lot of people become."

As all good Randy Travis fans know, Lib Hatcher, Randy's manager and wife, has been an overwhelming influence throughout much of Randy's life. To Martha, Lib's personality is a perfect complement to Randy's laid-back mien.

"I think that Lib is one of the most unusual women

I've met in my life. I've never in my entire life known anybody as focused as she is. Her focus is Randy and Randy's career and really, nothing else matters much. Twenty-four hours a day and seven days a week her focus is Randy's career. And she loves to work, loves the whole thing. I simply have never seen anybody who can juggle so many things. I told her one day that I have watched her, the first couple of years, go through the whole process of going from the bread truck [that they first used to drive to dates] to five buses or however many they've got, four, five, three, whatever; lots of buses; apartment buildings, houses. She supervised every fabric sample, every wallpaper sample. *Nothing* escapes her eye or her control. She wants it just right and she wants it right for Randy.''

In the course of their relationship, particularly before their marriage, a great deal of gossip and many stories were heard, forgettable stuff, but stuff, nevertheless.

''I think the situation that came up about their relationship in terms of the general public is unfortunate. Anytime you stay mysterious about things then people are gonna crucify you when they learn the truth, especially if it's something they're not comfortable with. And I don't care because I'm real comfortable with where they are right now. I have heard in some of the things he's written recently a real depth of feeling that I think has to do with their relationship. They're happy with it and that's all I care about.

''She's done a phenomenal job. He's said, 'She's the one with the drive.' He loves to sing and he loves to perform. And I do think that's important to him. But I think in a lot of respects he'd be just as happy out in Ashland City at his ranch with his horses, and I hope they're gonna slow up, but that's a very tough thing to do, especially at this stage of their career. He's got a big organization to support and it's very hard. It's a real Catch 22. But I know that everything she's done has been a labor of love for him.

"I remember early on, before they got their buses and stuff and they were flying, people were saying, 'Lib, you really ought to stay home and let Randy go [out and work] because you've got all this stuff to do here. You've set up this booking agency and your management company,' and that sort of stuff. And she said, 'You know, if Randy's gonna fly somewhere, I'm gonna fly somewhere because if the plane goes down with him, I want to be on it. There's no life for me without him.' And I have no doubt she feels that way."

Randy Travis is at a curious point in his career. One of the reasons his explosion onto the country scene gave birth to this whole country hunk movement was the tremendous sales impact his albums had. His sales are still respectable, but there are other, newer stars selling considerably more than Randy on their latest albums. How does Warner Brothers intend to take this man who means so much to them and bring his sales back up to where they were just a couple of short years ago when he was the hottest thing in country music?

"We would all love to have him back at double and triple platinum, and I don't know that we as a company can control that. What we can do is provide the best songs that we can for him, and the best production work, and the best marketing expertise that

we can come up with but the fact of the matter is that there are a lot of factors involved with the fact that he's not at the level he was.

"One is just normal: he was too hot not to cool down. He was just the only ball game in town back then. Now there's *lots* of other people for [record buyers] to spend their money on. I don't know how much effect bad publicity had on it; I suspect some but not that he couldn't overcome. I have had people out of the business comment about the marriage. But I don't really think that's it either. I think he needs a great hit record, a great song, and hopefully we found some for the *Greatest Hits* [album] and for the next album.

But, he may never get back to where he was. *Always And Forever* continues to outsell most other albums that we've got, and right now it's probably still outselling the current album. It will not quit. That was the career album. 'Forever And Ever Amen' is still his career record. I don't know that you can have two [career records]. I think he'll have a long career, like George Strait has.''

8

George Strait

NEARLY EVERYBODY IN THE COUNTRY MUSIC business today loves to say that, with new hot country hunks erupting every year, it's obvious that the competition is so great that hit-making careers are bound to be shortened.

Don't tell that to George Strait. In 1981, four years before Randy Travis came on the scene and kicked the country record business out of neutral into fourth gear, George Strait had his first number one record, "Unwound."

A dozen years later, his achievements include three gold and two platinum albums, eight number one singles, a near double platinum home video, and a big fistful of major recording industry awards. He still draws full houses in big concert halls. In Texas, which is where most of the *real* country fans are, he is sacred.

Two things about George Strait: (1) He will probably never have the multi-platinum sales that so many who followed him have had, and (2) he is a pretty good bet to still be having gold albums after the year 2000.

George Strait—first CMA Entertainer of the Year Award.

A note about country music: first, as almost everybody in the industry will tell you, it's "country," not "country and western." Country and western is an old term that was current in the days of the singing cowboys, when Roy or Gene or Tex could squeeze off thirty-seven shots from the ol' six gun without reloading, and then pick up a guitar and sing a song. Referring to country music as country and western is roughly equivalent to referring to black music as "race music." And yet many members of the media use this old terminology.

The only reason I bring all that up now is that, while the "western" in country and western so often sang idealized, romanticized and sanitized—often magnificently so—songs of the range, some of the grittiest, most honest western songs are sung by today's country singers. Garth Brooks's "Rodeo" comes to mind. And then, of course, there's George and "Amarillo By Morning," among others.

Among all the "hats," George is the one whose wide-brimmed Resistol cowboy hat really covers the head of a cowboy. Not so very remarkable, when you think about it. In Texas, Oklahoma, Wyoming, Colorado, Montana, and many other places, people rope calves on ranches. And so does George. Some of them have competed in a rodeo event built around that skill. And so has George. More remarkable is his career, which keeps on chugging along steadily at the rate of about one hit album a year, plus months of concerts in front of the fans who love him. And maybe, because he is not the biggest selling hunk out there, maybe because he does not get the daily press hype, they feel that much more strongly that he is *theirs*.

You might say that George Strait's audience isn't all that wide, but it's *very* deep.

George Strait got his first and, so far, only record deal with MCA Records. The man who signed him was none other than Jim Foglesong, who you may recall was head of Capitol Records in Nashville years later, when Garth Brooks walked into his office with a guitar. There are so many ways for an artist to come to the attention of a record label. This is one of them.

"Erv Woolsey had dropped out of the record business for a couple of years and owned a night club down in Texas," Foglesong remembers. "He befriended an act, who came in and worked his club, named George Strait. He also noticed that whenever George worked, why, the crowds were a little better. The way I remember it, George contacted Erv after Erv got back in the record business—we hired him as our Midwest regional promotion manager, working out of Chicago and then we brought him in to take the national job and moved him to Nashville.

"George contacted Erv and said that he really wanted to make an attempt to get a record deal, and get out of just working clubs in this little area of Texas. So he came into town and did a demo session, I believe, with producer Blake Mevis. They came in and played it for me, and very honestly I thought George sang really well but I didn't hear anything special. There are so many wonderful singers that come out of Texas. They're all over the place working in clubs down there. A person who's in A & R . . . will hear six or seven of these people a year at least, and sometimes fly down and see 'em."

Very often when an artist becomes a star he or she

will be able to point to this or that label who turned him or her down, and the audience at large wonders, "How could they have not known that he was a star?" Answer: you don't know who's a star until that person becomes a star. There's nothing inevitable about it. Often the artist has to meet the *right* label, the *right* management, the *right* producer, the *right* song, at the *right* time before the magic happens.

"Ron Chancey, who was the head of A & R, seemed to agree with me that, yes, he's very good, he's a likable guy, and all that. Erv told us about his success with George at the club, but we, I guess didn't hear any hits, and weren't motivated to sign him. George had been into town again and maybe even done another session . . . we were posted on it. Erv was his friend and giving him advice, and maybe he and Blake were pitching him around town to other labels after we had said no. But one afternoon, Ron Chancey came in and he said, 'You know, I think that this guy George Strait has something. I've been listening to that [his session] and I know I didn't hear him in the beginning but I think he's special.' I said, 'Sign him! That's all I'm waiting for.' I said, 'I'm not most comfortable with this particular type of artist anyway and I'm just waiting for somebody to come in excited. If you think we can have hits with him, let's sign him.'

"That's how the signing took place. Blake Mevis produced him. The first single was a wonderful song called 'Unwound.' I think it went to number one and right off the bat we had success with George. Sales kicked in—not immediately, it takes a while to establish [an artist] but it's really unusual to have a big huge single like that [so quickly] and they followed that with several really wonderful singles. I remember George calling me one day and wanted the company to lend him $25,000 to get a motor home. They didn't want a bus, but they'd been driving around in station wagons and cars and putting in a lot of mileage and they were in bad shape and they wanted a better mode of transportation. I had to go to bat for him with the hierarchy on the West Coast because record companies, whereas they are often giving artists advances and tour support, they're not in the banking business and giving loans; but at that time, why, I think he had extended his credit with the banks about as far as he could go. It was no big deal for the company to lend him this money which, I might add, got paid back very quickly.

"It was so exciting to see that whole process take place. George is a very low-key guy. He's a very bright guy . . . He's a real cowboy who can ride a horse. I think he was literally a foreman on a ranch when we signed him and he did clubwork on the side. He's a college graduate with a degree in agronomy."

With George's career off to a fast start he looked like money in the bank for MCA Records, and then, suddenly, it seemed, there was something wrong between him and his producer, Blake Mevis, which got the normally unflappable Mr. Foglesong extremely nervous.

"It's so difficult to have a winning combination that I'd do everything in the world to save that combination. [This falling out was apparently] over a selection of material [in the music business 'material' means 'songs'] and I can't remember all the details.

Blake was unhappy. George was unhappy. I tried every way in the world to get them to work together because I just didn't know what to do after that.''

Now, it's time to sympathize for a moment with this record executive whom nearly everybody on Music Row recognizes as an absolute prince of a fellow. This was not 1992, when a new country star is being discovered every few months. This was 1982, when the Urban Cowboy craze is fading, all too slowly, and nothing yet is taking its place. The only young acts really selling country records at this point are Alabama and Jim Foglesong's most heralded signing for MCA, George Strait. ''Please George, let's keep the team together. Please Blake, let's keep the team together,'' he might be saying. But the team is not staying together, and he's losing sleep wondering if George's career is flying right out the window over George's and his producer's failure to agree on songs to record.

''It was obvious that they were not going to be able to work together and there was no longer good communication. So, someone suggested that Ray Baker step in to produce George.''

Who is Ray Baker, you may well ask. Remember, throughout the 1970s and early eighties most country producers were going out of their way to make their records *not* sound too country. Mostly, except for Ray Baker. He was best known for some great Moe Bandy records, but he produced many successful country acts. You always knew that when Ray Baker took an artist into the studio, the record that resulted would be a genuine country record.

Ray took George into the studio and came out with

what would be George's first gold album, which in those difficult years was considered phenomenal. At this point the vicious politics of the music business took over. Jim Foglesong, Erv Woolsey, and a number of other individuals were gone from MCA, which hired the legendary and relentless Jimmy Bowen to run their Nashville division.

Woolsey became George Strait's manager and the two of them have built up a considerable empire that includes music publishing, stores, and numerous other ventures. Foglesong moved on to Capitol Records and the signing of Garth Brooks before Bowen caught up with him there too. Over a period of more than two decades the formidable Mr. Foglesong, whose record career started in the fifties in New York with Columbia/Epic, accomplished many great things. He survived every twist and turn of fortune in the record business—except for Jimmy Bowen.

George Strait's career cruised smoothly through the giant shakeup at MCA. Look at some of the awards he's won: Country Music Association's Entertainer of the Year, 1989 and 1990; Academy of Country Music's Entertainer of the Year, 1989; SRO Touring Artist of the Year, 1990; *Radio & Records* Country Performer of the Year Award, 1990; and American Music Awards Top Male Country Vocalist, 1991.

Where does George's career go from here? Probably the way it's been going for the past ten years, which is very very well. But Foglesong sees other interesting possibilities.

''I understand he's about to make a movie. We talked about that seven or eight years ago. He's a good looking guy, you know he looks *so* clean cut—

he has a *great* head of hair; you know, so many of the hat acts, and people in the past have receding hairlines or are totally bald, but George has one of the great heads of hair, probably the greatest head since Ronald Reagan. I always thought he was a natural for, for, maybe, a comeback of the cowboy movie.''

Earlier Foglesong mentioned George Strait's first single, ''Unwound,'' which became Strait's first number one hit. The song was written by two very dedicated *country* songwriters, Frank Dycus and Dean Dillon. Dillon is a talented writer/artist who has had a number of record deals. He would probably by now be as successful as an artist as he has been as a songwriter if he had not been so determined to do it all his way.

Dycus, a Kentucky boy, has been writing songs in Nashville for three decades. Years ago he too pursued a career as a recording artist, but he gave it up a long time ago. Songwriting is what he loves to do and his songs have been recorded by many of country's greatest. His biggest successes over the years have been the three hits he and his buddy Dillon wrote for George.

Frank got to know Strait over the years and had the opportunity to observe him.

"Early in 1981, Blake Mevis called me up and said, 'I'm doin' an artist. I'm doin' a spec.' " Now, what Blake was saying, in tech-talk, was that he was recording a singer for the purpose of getting him a record deal with a label.

Blake had heard several songs that Frank and Dean had written, and he said he wanted to cut them on this new artist. "I said, 'Well, cut 'em on him.'

"This one particular song [said Blake], 'Unwound', it just knocks me out."

"And I said, 'Well, you know, I was thinkin' about gittin' a Johnny Paycheck cut on that song but if you want to cut it go ahead and if the boy hits, I want some more cuts.' " Dycus was agreeing with Blake Mevis that "Unwound" was a special song, the kind of song a songwriter tries to pitch to a top artist so it will have a better chance to be a big hit. Since Dycus was letting Blake have the song for an unknown, something that can kill the value of the song for years to come if it doesn't do very well on the charts, he was hoping for future favors in return for the favor Dycus was doing for him.

"And he said, 'Well, shoot, we're gonna do him next week.' And so, he invited me and Dean over to the session and—well, Dean didn't even go to the session, I don't think. I went over and hung around and George [who was the brand new unknown artist, of course] just sang the fire out of 'em, you know, and so I just fell in love with him immediately. He's such a quiet unassuming sort of person. And we got to be pretty close friends. Whenever he'd come to Nashville, why, we'd try to get together ... sure enough, 'Unwound' hit.

"I would say that George is probably the most sincere person that I've ever been around that's 'a superstar'. But I think [our friendship] has to do with the fact that I got to know him before he became a superstar. Once you reach the status that George Strait is in now, it's almost impossible to make new friends. You're 'elevated' so high with your success that you've got tons and tons and tons of people that want to be friends with you just because of who you are, not what you are. And George is basically just a country boy, you know, hunts deer, and ropes calves. At the time I was runnin' pretty fast and loose. I was divorced and had just lost my family and all that and George had all the family ties and family 'goodies' that I was lookin' for or wanted—the stability—and just bein' around him kinda put *my* feet back on the ground, and let me know that there *is* a family life still alive. It was good for me. Slowed my life down an awful lot just bein' around George and his family.

"We wrote some together. And we went to Las

Vegas together, spent a week out there. I went down to San Marcos and went with him to gigs, out on the road. I enjoy Texas honky-tonks a lot. I've always enjoyed 'em. They're entirely different from what we call honky-tonks in Tennessee. It's more of a social event in Texas. I think you get a real good ear for what's happening in 'country' music by bein' there.

"I really got a preview of what George Strait was gonna be long, long before Nashville did. He'd play clubs like in Killeen, Texas, which would seat 600–700 people, and there'd be more people in the parking lot tryin' to get in than there'd be inside the club. It was just phenomenal. And you could come back to Nashville and tell them about it and they thought Texas was some foreign country. At that particular time, country music was still goin' in a pop direction, with no idea whatsoever of goin' back to basic country music.

"And George was cuttin', and performing Texas swing and traditional country songs, barroom songs and, basically just doin' what is really happenin' now. But he was, like, eleven years ahead of his time. And when you told people that there was more people in the parking lot tryin' to get in than there were inside the club, they'd look at you dumbfounded, cause, [they'd say] if he's so great, why would he be playin' a club? Cuz then it was super coliseums and package shows. *So* [when I saw how the fans loved George], I thought that country music was really gonna turn into what it is now, and I kept writing barroom songs and country songs, and my publisher, I'd bring 'em drinkin' songs and they'd say 'Don't bring me no

drinkin' songs, Frank! MADD mothers are bannin'
'em, you know.' ''

Frank Dycus and Dean Dillon cowrote three of
George's earliest key cuts: "Unwound," "Down And
Out," and "Marina Del Rey."

'' 'Marina Del Rey' was the biggy that just seemed
to bust George wide open," Dycus remembers with a
smile. "George asked me, 'All your songs, soon as
you demo, send 'em to Blake.' '' This meant that
George loved Dycus's and Dillon's songs so much
that he wanted the first shot at recording them. After
"Unwound" established George as a hitmaker, Dycus
was only too glad to comply because under normal
conditions it's very difficult to get a song recorded,
and with George "looking" for Dycus/Dillon songs,
Frank could feel that he had a singer who leaned toward his songs.

"He was getting ready for his second album, then.
We demoed five songs and took them to Blake and
Blake passed on them [turned them down]. In the
meantime, I flew to Fort Worth and met George at
Billy Bob's—we were gonna spend three or four days
together—and [when I told him we were coming] he
said, 'Well, didn't you demo last week?'

"I said, 'Yeah,' and he said, 'Well, bring it.'

"And I said, 'Your producer has already passed on
all of them,' and he said, 'Well, I wanna hear them
anyway.'

"We got in the car leavin' Fort Worth drivin' back
to San Marcos—George had drove up to this particular date in his own car because it was so close and
he put the tape in and 'Marina Del Rey' was the first
song on the tape. He played it and backed it up, and

played it and backed it up and played it and backed it up and played it and said, 'I'm gonna cut that song' after he played it the fourth or fifth time. Which was an absolute total shocker to me because it strayed so far from the honky-tonk barroom thing that he'd done before. He just immediately fell in love with the song. Basically what I think it is— most people don't know it, but, George Strait is a Frank Sinatra fan. He loves that kind of music— 'One For My Baby, One More For The Road,' 'Learnin' The Blues'—they're pop but they're still kind of a barroom—urban honky-tonk.

"George has always had a sense for material that I don't think any other artist I've ever met has. George don't know what he wants to do. He knows what he *don't* want to do and he knows what he likes when he hears it.''

''Marina Del Rey'' was an important song in the early part of George Strait's recording career. ''You still hear it all the time,'' smiles Dycus. Songwriters love *nothing* like they love hearing their songs on the radio.

''Marina Del Rey'' was a long way from what George normally likes to record and what his fans normally like to hear from him. ''I think Bob Wills influenced George more than anybody. If you go back and really listen to what Bob Wills did that was big band stuff. Those guys had horns, violins. . . beautiful smooth kind of music, ballroom dancing except with a different sound from Tommy Dorsey, say. Nashville is still not familiar with western swing.''

Dycus loves the steadiness of George Strait. ''Probably the easiest way to describe George Strait is to, say, look at his band. He's still got [almost all] the same guys that he started with, and that tells you something right there.'' That shows that his music hasn't changed much and, Dycus adds, ''He takes care of the people around him. These guys go back to his college days.''

Unlike almost all the other hunks in this book, George Strait was not raised to make music. Born near Poteet, Texas, in 1952, he was the son of a math teacher. He didn't spend his Saturday nights on the living room floor with the family listening to the Grand Ole Opry and he didn't have a guitar made from a cigar box with the strings pulled out of an old screen door. In fact, the family didn't have a record player and when his dad turned on the radio, it was the news or the farm reports he listened to.

His family did have a cattle ranch in West Texas so, if anything, George was raised to be a cowboy.

In high school he did some singing in the local bands—the standard rock repertoire—and after high school he ran away to Mexico with his high school sweetheart. Across the Rio Grande, they were married, and they're still married.

He did some restless time at Southwest Texas State University before beginning a three year tour of duty in the army that took him to Hawaii. Now, what happened in Hawaii is the kind of serendipity that always happens to someone else, right? George had always wanted to be a country singer, and, according to one *Country Music* magazine article, out in Hawaii, half a world away from West Texas, the base commander had an impulse to organize a country band.

So George applied himself to learning what country singers must know. He sent away for sheet music of songs recorded by his favorite artists—Jones and Haggard, of course, and Hank Williams—and set about learning to play guitar.

After leaving the army, he went back to Southwest Texas State to pursue a degree in agricultural education, but the course he was really charting led elsewhere. He and his band were playing the local clubs around San Marcos, the way Garth Brooks later did at Oklahoma State.

Unlike most of the other hunks, it had taken him a while to start his dreamchase, but now he was in hot pursuit, even though the goal was too distant to provide him with any real hope. He had a family now, and after graduation the days were too short. He was putting in long hours managing a cattle ranch and long nights playing dance halls and parties. He'd take an occasional trip to Nashville, feeling out the music business and getting little response in return. By 1979, he later told *Country Music*, "I was just fixin' to go ahead and quit. I was twenty-seven years old, I'd been playing for six or seven years, and I was beginning to think I just wasn't good enough and maybe ought to try something else. I gave my band notice and signed up for a full-time job with this outfit in Uvalde, Texas, that designed cattle pens. But a week before I was to report for the job, I realized that I just couldn't do it. And I decided to give it one more year."

We'll never know if George would have given up the dream for good if he hadn't accomplished anything in the music business during that year. Not long after, his and Erv Woolsey's paths crossed at the Prairie Rose, the club Erv was running in San Marcos.

Let's think about this for a minute. San Marcos, Texas, is a community of about twenty thousand people. George Strait is singing in a club during the relatively short time that it is being run by the one man within a week's pony ride of George's world who has the savvy and experience to help establish George in the record business. George's short forays into Nashville before he met Erv indicate that he didn't quite have the brassy nerve to bring his family to Nashville and get beat up there for five or ten years hoping for a break.

But because their paths did cross in San Marcos, we have George Strait. Lucky for George. Lucky for Erv. Lucky for us. Which brings up some interesting questions. Would we have a George Strait without an Erv Woolsey? Would we have a Randy Travis without a Lib Hatcher? Would we have a Garth Brooks without a Bob Doyle? As talented as these artists are, the answer may well be no. Success is what happens when talent meets opportunity, and often managers provide the opportunity. It is common for the media to write about successful performers as if they carried the load themselves. Managers and agents are often depicted as leeches. In fact, success in the music business is nearly always a team effort. Sometimes a hit-making career is born because the artist meets his future manager in a San Marcos night club. Sometimes a hit-making career is born because an artist, or his producer, finds the perfect song at the perfect time. Sometimes, believe it or not, a hit-making career is born because a session musician improvises the perfect instrumental lick for making a hit record.

More often, a hit-making career is *not* born, because a talented artist did *not* come across the right manager, or the right song, or the right lick, when his career really needed it.

One of the best things to happen to country music happened at the Prairie Rose. George Strait is among the great stars in the history of country music and of all the hunks tearing up the country record business today, George was there first.

9

Clint Black

NOBODY TALKS ABOUT IT, BUT THERE'S A HUNK race going on out there. It's much like a horse race, only it lasts a lot longer, and no matter who is leading right now, a year or two or three down the track someone else is going to take the lead.

Back in the eighties, for instance, Randy Travis had a big lead over the field. A year and a half ago, Garth Brooks took command and looked unbeatable. Then along came Billy Ray Cyrus with the fastest selling debut album in the history of country music. Travis Tritt and Alan Jackson are battling hard among the leaders. You can see Vince Gill making a move along the rail, and behind him, coming up smartly, is Mark Chesnutt, challenging the veterans.

The fun part is trying to figure out which of these horses is going to make the next big move. Some people believe that Travis Tritt, whose *It's All About To Change* album has achieved double platinum status, will soon be challenging for the lead. Tracy Lawrence, Aaron Tippin, and Doug Stone all have their boosters who believe they can make it to the front of the field. There are even a few who say that

Marty Stuart's tours with Travis Tritt will be the match that ignites the fuse of that little keg of dynamite. And then, of course, there's always the chance that the next monster hunk is playing in a club somewhere, just about to pack and head for Middle Tennessee.

But in the middle of this past summer, one of the former leaders made a giant move toward the front. We hadn't heard much from Clint Black for awhile because of a little career glitch, but in July RCA put out his first album in many, many months. It debuted on the pop album chart in the number ten slot, and the evidence indicates that Clint might be even hotter than ever. Until Billy Ray, nobody, ever, in country music started hotter than Clint started. He still had his momentum when his troubles began, and there's now no reason in the world to believe that the magic has disappeared.

In the early part of 1989, RCA released Clint's first single, "A Better Man." It shot up the charts to number one in the key trade magazines and *Billboard* announced that he was the first male country artist in fifteen years to go number one with his debut single.

That wasn't the amazing part. The debut album, *Killin' Time*, came out in May and took less than six months to go platinum. Five number one singles came off the album, which itself stayed number one on the country album charts for thirty-one weeks. Most people don't remember that Clint and Garth broke out of the starting gate at about the same time and that, early on in that race, Clint flat beat Garth's brains out.

So what happened? Why did we have to wait so long for Clint's new album, wondering if all his old

Clint Black—1989 CMA Horizon Award.

fans were still waiting too? More on that later. First, let's get a producer's eye view of Clint Black.

Mark Wright came to Nashville while still a teenager. Success as a songwriter came fairly quickly for him, but what really caught the ears of a number of music business people was the quality of the demos he was producing. By the time he was into his midtwenties he had a job producing records for RCA. He had come a long way in a short time, but he needed a hit act.

"I was doing A & R for RCA when a tape came across my desk from my boss at the time, Joe Galante. He told me to listen to the tape and get back to him. I listened to it and the songs were just real fresh. I loved the tape, got back to Joe and said, 'This is a killer, let's go see this guy.' Come to find out he's managed by Bill Ham [who managed the big pop act, Z.Z. Top]. We went down to Houston to see him play at a place called Rockefeller's, I believe, and he was just a charming, good looking kid, you could tell that he was really smart. He could carry on a real good conversation—he wasn't like, a brainless hillbilly singer. And you listen to his songs, you could tell he had some intellect. His lyrics were pretty well crafted. Everybody who went down, marketing people, promotion guys, myself and Joe, and James Stroud [who produces an impossible number of hit artists and usually produces them very well]. I thought, this guy's got his act together for a young kid, writin' great songs like this. We just went back and signed him, and made a record.

"And used his band. His band was a killer. Awesome. So we actually cut him in Houston. And came back to Nashville and finished up the overdubs.''

Nashville record producers almost never use an artist's band, especially on the first album. Critics like to point that out as evidence of Nashville's desire to squelch the creativity of artists. In fact, most live bands have a tendency to overplay, which is fine when you're trying to fire up a dance crowd in a skull orchard. But session musicians are more likely to lay down the simple, solid tracks that wear well when played repeatedly on the radio.

And yet, RCA allowed Clint Black, who had never had a major record released, to work with his own band right from the beginning. Why?

"Clint," continues Mark, "is just one of those guys who knows what he wants. And his band was great. They're all great, but he had a particularly good steel player, Jeff Peterson—I mean he could be in Nashville doing studio work all the time if he lived here. The band was great and Clint felt comfortable with it.''

When music people started hearing his songs, it became obvious that he didn't write like most of Nashville's career songwriter crowd.

"He writes about a lot of true-life experiences. Staff writers [for the big publishing companies] in this business, they write *so* many songs and they have to fictionalize so much and so, [they tend to repeat] a lot of the same subjects. But when you're writin' about a lot of your own stuff, you know, that you really feel, then it becomes personalized and so it becomes unique.''

So how did he get so good and unique, so young?

"My opinion," suggests Mark, "is that this is just a guy that studied it, wanted it—and that's a very big [term] 'wanted it.' And he played a lot of 'happy hours' with a guitar, sittin' out there, so he learned how to communicate with people up front. When you sit there with just a guitar and maybe a little drum machine or bass machine or whatever, I don't know what all he, I never saw him in that form, and you're sittin' there in front of forty people every night, or fifty people, or sixty people, you just learn how to communicate. And I think that comes across very well on television for him cuz you feel like he really knows how to talk to that camera, just like it was a guy sittin' right here next to him. To me he is *the* best on television as far as interviews. . . when he gets on TV you just feel like he's your buddy."

After the RCA gang came back from seeing Clint in Houston, the label signed him quickly, and they were anxious to get him into the studio.

"Yeah, we got into it. We got down, you know, everybody's sittin' around seein' the success of Randy Travis and George Strait, and RCA didn't have a hat act, and now we got one, let's hurry up and get him out [to the public]." And they did.

"It was the first debut album in the history of recorded music, in the history of any music, Beatles, Elvis, anybody, to have five number one records on it."

Now that they finally had their first hat act (Clint's hat, by the way, is described by *People* as "a felt custom job by the Standard Hat Works in Waco, Tex."), what was RCA's first hint that something really phenomenal was about to happen for them?

"I swear, I think this had a lot to do with it but, maybe not. He did a Bob Hope special and he set on this boat, cruising through . . . somewhere, singing 'Better Man' and he did an interview with Bob Hope and Bob Hope loved him, man—one of Bob Hope's big specials. It seems like the week after that, he sold like a hundred thousand records. The album went gold on the first single." That's an incredibly fast public response to a brand new artist.

"The way he came across on TV, at that point, look at him and you go, 'This is Roy Rogers!' This guy's every mother's dream! You know he's just so lovable lookin'."

Normally, when a new artist comes on the scene, producers and A & R directors start calling up publishers and key writers all over Nashville, asking or begging them for great material. "I know this guy is new," they'll say. "But we believe he's gonna be a great new artist, and wouldn't you like to be the one to write (or publish) his first big hit?" Publishers and writers like to save their best songs for established hit acts with guaranteed built-in album sales and airplay, so it takes a crafty record producer to find great songs for a new act.

Clint Black's producers had no such problems. They heard the songs he had written and never even tried to find songs from outside songwriters or publishers. Thus all songs on his *Killin' Time* album were cowritten by Clint Black.

Looking for songs for Clint Black to record, says Mark, "Would be like telling Merle Haggard to cut an outside song [early in his career]. Part of what makes him an artist is his songwriting. His style is so unique as a writer... what the public wants is him. It's an expression of what he is, so there was really no need to look for outside songs. There were thirty of his songs on the tape he gave us. We felt that we should be the objective ear to make the decisions [of which of those songs to record]. Of course if there were some that Bill Ham just absolutely had to have on there that he loved, or that Clint absolutely loved and had to have on there, they let us know that—so we didn't miss it."

Once again, this is a radical departure from the way Nashville used to do business. Twenty years ago, new artists were generally told what songs they should record. In fact, many veteran artists were told what they should record. Only powerful artists like Elvis in his later years or Conway Twitty exercised control over their material. There were power struggles between producers and artists, but they were relatively rare. A surprising number of country artists regarded it as the producer's job to find songs to record. And the producers were only too glad to oblige, sometimes writing the songs, or publishing the songs, or relying on their good buddies to provide songs to feed to their artists.

The story is that Willie and Waylon, more than anybody else, made Nashville start to change their ways. These two very independent personalities felt that Nashville, stuck deep in a rut of mediocrity, stood between them and the kind of music they needed to perform. They insisted on the right to control their own music, and they had the force to make it stick.

Since then, more and more Nashville record executives have come to believe that the artist, even a brand new artist, should have a decisive voice in choosing the music he records. Under that new way of thinking, country has grown so powerful that country artists will probably have a strong voice in their recording careers for many years to come.

Clint's first album was unusual in another way. Today it's very common for country artists to "overcut," that is, record more songs than they intend to put on the album. So an artist might cut twelve to fifteen or even more songs for a ten song album. That way, if one song seems a little weak, and another song doesn't quite come off in the studio, the label still has other songs to choose from to insure a high quality album. But according to Mark Wright, they didn't work that way on Clint's album.

Tanya Tucker congratulates Clint.

"I believe we cut ten songs," he says. "We put nine on the cassette [several years ago RCA's then-Nashville-head Joe Galante decreed that there would be only nine songs on RCA country albums] and the CD had all ten on it."

It was as if the label had supreme confidence in the entire package that was Clint Black. His voice, his personality, his band, his songs, and his manager; there was no doubt this man was going to be a big star. If they really felt that way, well, how right they were!

And if they felt that way, maybe they picked up that confidence from Clint himself.

"He knows what he wants," Mark Wright repeats. "He looks at a spot on the wall, aims at it, and hits it. And he gets everybody around him to help him hit that spot. This guy is pretty driven."

Okay, he's driven. But Mark Wright and James Stroud are professional producers, and Clint Black was recording for national distribution on a major record label for the first time. How did those sessions work? Did the professionals just sit back and let the music happen?

"The main thing I would do is change tempos," Wright recalls. "And Stroud would get in and change drum sounds, and go out and tune the drums. A lot of times the arrangement would be a little too busy, you know, you really hope the song'll jump out. The production on this is a lot different than on a lot of things. A lot of things you have to create. This was pretty created when we got there. All we had to do is just put a little icing and a little shimmy and shine and shimmer."

Once all the tracks are recorded on a session, they are carefully combined in something called a "mix." In the stereo world of modern recording, a mix is more than just how loud the vocal is compared to the guitar, compared to the bass, compared to the drums. And it's more than the amount of echo or treble or bass added or subtracted. A stereo mix may construct a stage in the mind—or ears—of the studio engineer and the producer, so that a knowledgeable listener can close his or her eyes and imagine the stage and the location of all the performers on that stage. The effect can be striking. Obviously the mix can be very important to the success of a record. So just who was responsible for the mix on that fabulous RCA debut album of Clint Black?

"That's another story," laughs Mark. "We had different versions of these mixes." He laughs some more. "We had different groups go in [to the control room] and do 'em. We had Bill Ham and Clint; and James and me. I can honestly say . . . there were just a lot of versions."

And whose versions wound up on the record?

"I'm not gonna say," he replies.

It's fairly obvious that Clint Black was not exactly awed by the hotshot Nashville music veterans he was working with.

Not in the least, Wright agrees. "He'd get mad at me for puttin' a background vocal lick on the record that he didn't like. And he'd just get mad, and, get upset and, he wasn't scared of anything or anybody. He had his spot on the wall, like I said, and he was gonna hit it. I was just lucky to be there and be a part of it."

Clint Black with former Oak Ridge Boy Bill Golden

Did he spend much time with Clint during this time?

"Not really—a little bit. We'd go out and hang out a little bit. I told somebody one time, 'If I'd known he was gonna be that big, I'd a hung out with him every minute I could.' " That's the songwriter in Mark Wright talking. Not long after the album was finished, Mark and RCA came to a parting of the ways. After helping to launch the fastest rising star in the history of country music (up to that time), Mark was out on the street, professionally speaking. But he had a good track record, plenty of talent, and friends in the business who knew what he could do. Through the good offices of Tony Brown at MCA records,

Mark got a shot at another brand new Texas act, Mark Chesnutt. Again Mark Wright struck gold with a debut album. It was kind of funny, Wright recalls, to be leaving the company just as Clint's career was shooting skyward, but, he smiles, "It was a little easier to leave if you had a platinum record under your arm."

Now, how hot can a new artist get? By October, 1990, about a year and a half after it was released, that first album soared past the two million sales mark. His second album, *Put Yourself In My Shoes*, came out in November and within weeks *it* was platinum. Those first two albums would accumulate combined sales of five million plus, the fastest start in the history of country music until Clint's contemporary, Garth Brooks, kicked into gear and left everybody in the dust. Meanwhile, he was getting great exposure touring with Alabama, but he was already so hot that he began headlining shows himself and drawing large, enthusiastic crowds. Less than two years after the RCA scouting team saw Clint performing in Texas, he was the hottest young act country music had ever experienced.

Clint's RCA bio tells us a bit about his early musical career.

"The youngest of four musical sons, Clint took full advantage of his brothers' performing experience. With the encouragement of his parents, he began performing with his brothers at the family's 'Country Sunday on Saturday' backyard barbecues, which were derived from Houston's 'Country Sunday' celebrations in the early 70s. 'I was too young to go to the real thing, so we held our own,' he recalls. 'They'd go all night long, and when my brothers took a break I'd sit on a stool in the middle of the yard and keep going.' "

By the time he graduated from high school he was absolutely hooked on performing and by 1981 he was playing the Houston club circuit. When singers start working the local clubs, that's often the make or break time for them.

The club circuit can wear a performer down. Singing before drinking customers who are shouting conversations to each other over the noise of his most soulful deliveries is demoralizing. Instead of having fun entertaining folks, he finds himself slipping into the deadly routine of background music for a hundred dollars a night.

But for one who is ambitious, talented, and tough, the local club circuit is the opportunity for him to hone his skills, to develop a distinctive vocal style and learn to work an audience. A tough audience is a challenge. If he can win over a bunch of sour-faced drunks who came to blow off steam, then entertaining a concert hall full of dedicated fans will be a breeze.

Six years on the Houston club circuit not only sharpened Clint's musical chops, but put him in touch with Hayden Nicholas, who was to become his most frequent cowriter. This was also the period when Clint had the experiences that inspired so many of those thirty or so songs that would later impress Mark Wright and his associates.

As his skills developed, along with his local reputation, Clint felt he was ready to take a shot at the big time. Somehow Clint had grasped an idea that even many experienced Nashville music people did not understand: that if he could find himself a really good manager, then he would have a much better chance of getting the record deal he craved. He happened to know about a big time manager in Houston, Bill Ham, who managed and produced the major rock act Z.Z. Top. Clint made a tape of some of those Black/Nicholas songs and undertook a campaign of finding the right person who could get the tape to Ham. Eventually he found that man, and when Ham heard the tape, it turned out that he was looking for a country act. Clint seemed to fill the bill. So he got in touch with Clint and asked him up for a meeting.

In Ham's office, with a guitar, he wove the same magic as Garth Brooks wove for Jim Foglesong. Good managers know what to do when they find the right talent. Within a matter of days, Clint was in Nashville meeting with RCA executive Joe Galante. As Mark Wright related earlier, from then on events moved very quickly.

But the very power that allows a manager to launch the career of an artist can cause fear and loathing on the part of that artist. "Is he acting in my best interests or his?" "Is most of the money going into my pocket, or his?" "Does he intend to squeeze me dry then throw me away?" Show business jokes about managers and agents are endemic: "When I donate at the local blood bank my manager always goes with me to take his ten percent," etc., etc. Sometimes the

artist's suspicions are justified. Sometimes they are not.

So Clint and the man who got his career on track separated. Clint's public remarks about Ham were unkind, to say the least. Ham's public comments were considerably more restrained. The truth is difficult for an outsider to untangle. *Billboard* columnist Ed Morris did his best to try in a column segment subheaded "Dueling Press Releases," parts of which are included below.

In March of 1992, Clint released a statement through his publicist, saying, in part, "Since I was inexperienced in the business aspects of the entertainment industry, I put my trust and faith in Bill Ham and expected that he would always act in my best

interest." Ham, he continued, took commissions beyond those provided by their agreement, didn't provide him with full and timely business information,
and then made himself scarce when Clint wanted to
meet with him.

Clint's statement came through Jonni Hartman of
T. J. Hartman Public Relations. Jonni Hartman happens to be Clint's mother-in-law, and it was she
who took the principal shots from Ham's public
response.

" . . . So, when I read Jonni Hartman's . . . press release, I cannot believe in my heart that Clint had anything to do with it, as I consider the attack unworthy
of him."

Black, he insisted, "is not only a talented performer, but . . . has a keen intelligence and a shrewd
calculating mind for business." Ham follows with an
assertion that his company has done a proper job of
representing Clint.

In the course of this struggle, which included ex-
tensive legal proceedings involving Black, Ham, and
RCA, Clint's recording career suffered.

His public had been crying for a new album but it
wasn't until the spring of 1992 that Black and RCA
managed to resolve any conflicts they had with each
other. Shortly thereafter the label announced a new
contract, which was directly with Clint, unlike the
original contract, which was with Ham. The album,
titled, *The Hard Way*, was released in July. The folks
must have been waiting on pins and needles for this
album, and RCA must have really had their sales and
marketing together. *The Hard Way* took the easy way
into the top ten on the pop charts, proving that after

a year and a half without a new album, Clint hadn't lost a step.

It's easy to remember that Garth Brooks has ruled the country album charts in recent times, and easy to forget that *Killin' Time* put Clint Black at the top of those charts for seven solid months. Now that Black is back, Garth, Travis Tritt, Alan Jackson, and the rest will have him to contend with. Of course, country stars generally deny that they are in direct competition with each other. But I guarantee you their management knows how much the competition is selling from week to week, what their concert price is, and which of them are hot on the video channels.

Clint Black has an enormous attraction for women of all ages. We haven't begun to see what Clint Black can accomplish in the world of country music.

10

Ricky Van Shelton

PEOPLE WHO DON'T UNDERSTAND COUNTRY MUSIC and have heard Ricky Van Shelton's hits have a hard time understanding how he fits with all other hunks.

Some people who don't listen think that because he wears a straw Resistol cowboy hat, and is selling a lot of records, he must sound like Randy Travis and Dwight Yoakam and all the other note-benders.

But folks who have heard Ricky Van on his singles, at least, know he's mostly a straight ahead crooner. "What's he doing in with those other guys?" people who don't understand will ask.

The answer is, that no matter how powerful the dominant trend, country music is always moving in several directions at once. For years now, Restless Heart has been pumping out hits, most of which sound more like seventies mainstream pop than the music most people identify as country. And back in the early sixties, when Patsy Cline was scoring with one major hit after another, her delivery was closer to that of pop stars like Jo Stafford or Kay Starr than Kitty Wells.

But in fact, on his hit singles, Ricky Van Shelton is just as much a new traditionalist as Randy Travis or George Strait. It's just that he is heir to a different country tradition. Randy's tradition is the Lefty Frizzell-Merle Haggard school. George's tradition, or at least one of them, draws heavily on Bob Wills-Ernest Tubb type music.

But there's another country tradition that people don't talk about much today. That's the straight ahead country crooner tradition, and it has an honorable history. Country crooners specialize in love ballads, slow or medium tempo love songs that may be positive or negative but generally don't have the barroom edge that make your regular honky-tonk ballads so appealing to hard-core country fans. Eddy Arnold was doing them in the fifties and thereafter. Jim Reeves broke the bank with them in the early sixties. After his death the country record industry hungered for a successor, but the closest they got was Ray Price, who abandoned his role as the best Texas country singer of his time in order to recycle himself into a country crooner. Marty Robbins was another whose style sometimes moved into the area of the pop-style love ballad.

Ricky Van Shelton is closer to Marty Robbins than to Jim Reeves. He is a great singer, with a wonderful range, and a way with old country ballad. And he has revived some great old country ballads. Many of them have been big hits, and Ricky Van Shelton's albums consistently sell platinum.

His entry into the wild-eyed dream of commercial

country music centers around four people, his wife
Bettye, a Nashville journalist named Jerry Thompson,
record producer Steve Buckingham, and recording executive Rick Blackburn.

Blackburn tells the story.

Ohio-born Blackburn is vice president and general
manager of Atlantic Records. In 1986 he was vice
president and general manager of CBS Records.
"Down here we just recycle record executives," says
Blackburn wryly. What he's referring to is the fact
that, since New York and California label chiefs don't
necessarily know who the best music people in Nashville are, they often replace their fired country executives with somebody else's fired executives.

"I brought a guy into the company [CBS] named
Steve Buckingham, who was a producer from California, originally from Atlanta . . . hired him as an
A & R executive. Steve and I were consciously looking for somebody who could penetrate George Strait's
market. George Strait at that time pretty much had the
upside of the market to himself. [This was before
Randy Travis]. Strait had had a phenomenal couple
of years. Good lookin' guy. Fit a profile that all of
our testing market research was showing [had] mass
appeal. I really set out to try to get somebody we
thought fit the profile that we could penetrate some of
that market.

"We looked at maybe six, seven, eight acts that
sort of fit that profile, and coincidentally, Jerry
Thompson, an old friend, not in the music business—
Jerry's in the newspaper business—came into my office and said that, through a fishing buddy or a
drinking buddy or something, 'I know of this guy in

Ricky Van Shelton

Grit, Virginia, wherever that is. You need to see him.' But he had a demo tape which was awful. I still have it around here, it was cut on a Wallensack, you know an old tape recorder—I mean, it was miserable, probably one of the all-time top ten worst demos that you could ever—you could barely hear the vocal. I kinda dismissed that, I couldn't tell anything, and Jerry was persistent.''

A word or two about the persistent Jerry Thompson: Thompson is one of Nashville's best loved journalists. A beefy, good-natured guy, he looks like a southern good ol' boy, a persona that years ago helped him penetrate the Ku Klux Klan. The result was a series of feature articles in the *Tennessean*, Nashville's morning paper, that won him a number of prestigious journalism awards. He has a regular column in that paper. He writes wonderful human interest pieces that are avidly read by thousands of devoted followers. Among his most interesting subjects is his long battle with cancer. His stories on that subject are low-key, devoid of self-pity, and filled with the kind of observant objectivity that has made Thompson an excellent reporter. It's not surprising that he got involved in launching the career of a struggling artist. Jerry Thompson is the kind of man who gets involved.

Blackburn continues.

''Ricky Van Shelton wouldn't fly. Probably still doesn't. He had a fear of flying. I believe through Jerry, they talked him into moving up here. I want to say he was a plumber, or a pipefitter, or something like that by trade and played music on the weekend like a lot of people do. I believe he left his job in Virginia and moved up here on a whim, trying to get something going. Bettye, his wife, got a job to support them and Jerry, persisting with me, finally walked this guy in the door, just walked him in, very shy, but sure had the look, really did have the look; [I] didn't know if he could sing a lick. I suggested that we put him on the stage of a bar around town. Didn't matter which one, I just wanted to see him on stage, try to get a feel for what he was, what kind of stage presence he had.

"So, I wanna say, we put him on the stage at the Stockyard." Now, the Stockyard is one of Nashville's best known restaurants, owned by Buddy Killen, who for many years was one of Nashville's most successful song publishers and record producers. The Stockyard has a celebrated dance hall/bar and listening room known as the Bullpen Lounge. It was there that Blackburn says Ricky gave his fateful audition.

"He sat in with a house band down there, and did a few songs . . . Ricky does not boast himself to be a songwriter, like so many of them do . . . he did 'covers.' And knocked us out. He really had a presence about him. He could sing a power ballad, he had some range to him. He had a very innocent stage presence, wasn't showy or goey . . . a very sincere innocent approach and wasn't trying to knock anybody over, but he was magnetic. So we flipped out and signed him.

"Well, Buckingham was with me, and he flipped out too. Then we proceeded to more or less draw the project up on a blackboard, a market segment that we were gonna shoot for; and it was not a George Strait approach but he had a look and at that point in time I felt that the look meant a lot. Video was coming in.

That young, good-looking guy was attracting the female buyer. It was a perfect marriage [Ricky and video].

"Don't forget, country music was just coming out of the era of shooting ourselves in the foot with this sugarcoated quote country. We would sign acts . . . and say, well, our real plan is to cross 'em over. And none of that worked. It's true. You're looking at one of them who took that position. Hell, we all did. Why? Because we're all stupid."

There were two reasons, Blackburn says, that during the early eighties the Nashville music industry ignored real country music in favor of sugarcoated country.

"One is that we got hung up on the statistics of the pop market, which was a whopping fifty-five percent of the industry, with country being less than ten. We thought if we were really gonna be successful, then we've got to be a player in the pop market as well as, then, the international market, so, just about every label had a candidate for that. Or two or three. The first time out we tried Rodney Crowell through that market. Rosanne through that market. Well, you can only be rejected so much. It's like a mule. You get hit upside the head and you [get to thinking], well, wait. We're going nowhere with this. I had reversed the position. I thought, well, let's set out to be the best that we can be at country music. For a change, let's try and make some great country records. Let's have an act that is appealing [to country fans]. Let's have an act that can carry us through the future for the next five years, five years being a 'future' for the record business.

Ricky Van Shelton and Dolly Parton

"So we consciously reversed our strategy. We were actively looking at that time. I think within a short period of time I signed four acts: Ricky Van Shelton, Marty Stuart, Sweethearts of the Rodeo, and a group called the O'Kanes. All of them pretty much country, the O'Kanes being pretty much a folk approach to country. To be honest with you, I really thought the one that would emerge out of there first was Marty Stuart. I really did. He had the look and pizzazz. But in reality Ricky Van Shelton did.

"Steve Buckingham and I worked on a strategy for the album, then set about finding some songs. The strategy originally had a little more rockabilly to it.

And if you go back to listen to that first record [album] we slanted it that way.

"[But] We had a song Joe Chambers wrote called 'Somebody Lied.' He had written that song for George Jones. That was the third single on the album. Now that's what you would call a career record, and it was a power ballad . . . we did a song . . . either the first or second song called 'Crime Of Passion'—we got the song out of Muscle Shoals, Alabama, but it was originally pitched to us for Marty Stuart. Marty didn't like the song. Marty cut it, and it didn't come off. Usually if an artist doesn't like a song, it won't come off very well. So we ran the song back around and did it on Ricky. I don't think Ricky was real high on it. But it enabled us to make a pretty good video, we showed him off pretty well in it. And then we felt the power of the tube.

" 'Somebody Lied' was [supposed to be] the third single; we did a video on that and it 'put away' the album. It went platinum. It was an explosion. We had one song scheduled to be a single that was written by two guys named Foster and Lloyd and they took the demo and went over to RCA, got a record deal, and released that as a first single so that took one away from us.

"But 'Somebody Lied' was a big ol' power ballad and I can remember our promotion department trying to talk us out of it, saying, 'Well, it's slow and it's draggy and radio's not gonna like it, we need to stay with something up in tempo.' " It might be worth commenting here that country radio, especially in the big cities where the competition among stations is great and the financial stakes are high, is very much into maintaining a fast paced musical format. They prefer fast or medium tempo records to slow love ballads. Paradoxically, many of the great classic hits, the ones that the folks really love and remember, are some of those very love ballads that radio is reluctant to play, especially when the artist is unknown.

"Buckingham and I put our foot down. Let's go [with 'Somebody Lied']. We don't have that much of a risk. Really showed us a lot about the marketplace and that there is a place for power ballads as long as you have a guy who can sing 'em. It really showed Ricky as an artist. It was a good song. So then we were off to the races. Next thing you know you've got a platinum album, and his career is well on its way. But some of that stuff happens by accident because if Foster and Lloyd had not gotten a record deal, chances are that their song would have been the next single." Then Ricky would have still been doing up tempo songs and CBS might not have discovered that Ricky Van Shelton doing beautiful ballads sells millions of cassettes and CDs.

"A lot of the stuff in this business is timing and luck, you know," smiles Blackburn, who can afford to smile because even as he speaks his young artist on Atlantic, Tracy Lawrence, is closing in on a gold album, early enough in the album's life that Blackburn is certain it will go platinum later.

"Next thing you know, his [Ricky's] career is blossoming. He's getting ten thousand dollars a night on the road—his career really exploded. I only had one other act in recent years whose career took off like that and that was Ricky Skaggs—similar kind of thing, different approach—Skaggs is more bluegrass, but different. I mean it was old stuff that people thought was new and fresh. This was an old Stanley Brothers approach. It's funny how that goes down, perception, you know?''

Not long after Van Shelton broke big, Sony bought CBS, and not long after that, Rick Blackburn was between labels. But the pattern was set. Ricky's first four LPs all went platinum, largely on the strength of the power ballads like the one that first launched his career. That fourth LP, *Backroads*, almost made it to the top of the country album charts and has demonstrated that he is just as powerful a country force today as he was last year, or the year before that.

Blackburn was, as we have noted, initially taken by Ricky's ''look,'' and later by his stage appearance and delivery. But he was also caught by Ricky's voice, in very subtle ways.

''He was to me, sort of like 'Marty Robbins lives.' He was a tenor, had a lot of range to him, and always had an innocent voice. He also had what we call a 'cue' about him. Superstars will walk into a room and radiate. Dolly Parton walks in you know she's a star, she doesn't have to tell you, you understand. Johnny Cash is bigger than life. And Ricky could do that. He could walk into a room as an unknown and never utter a word, and people were enamored with him. He really had a magnetic personality, complemented by an accent which he brought up from Virginia, which I thought was intriguing. He's also a very smart boy. He would ask the right questions, he had high morals about him, and he had a kind of sense of himself. You know you look for that when you sign an artist. You don't want to make somebody [into something] they're not. When somebody walks in here who's a pretty good singer and says, 'Hey, I can do anything you want me to do, I can be anything you want me to be,' you show him the door because they're not gonna have any kind of personality that you can market. They'll be a clone of something.

"Shelton was not a clone of anything. He was unique. The way he would look at issues. He was at peace with himself. He wasn't saying things he thought you wanted to hear. There were some songs we would bring to the table [when they were choosing his songs for the first album] and he would say, 'You know, that's not me. I don't feel comfortable singing that song. I mean I will if you want me to, but I just feel it's not me.' Fair enough. As opposed to an artist saying, 'Yeah, I love it,' tellin' [us] what we want to hear, and then you go into the studio and nothing happens [because] the singer really *didn't* feel good [about the songs]. He was fun to work with; he would work with you.

"He has a style, it's a 'no frills' style," notes Blackburn, referring to Ricky's straight ahead vocal delivery, so devoid of the note-bending we associate with artists like George Jones, Merle Haggard, and many of Ricky's contemporary hunks. "He doesn't try to be anything that he's not. He knows instinctively how to hold a note, where to emphasize. It really helps, like so many, if he genuinely likes a song. He'll give you a great vocal performance. You can count on that. Now, whether the song's a hit or not is another matter."

Then there's that Ricky Van Shelton image. Of all the hunks, none has an image more memorable than

Ricky Van Shelton in his straw cowboy hat and undershirt. The hat came with Ricky from Virginia. The undershirt, that was something else.

"That was our idea—Buckingham, myself, and probably Mary Ann McReady, as the product manager. We were playing around at a photo shoot with different wardrobes. 'Let's try this.' I think he was shy about it. But we also did a tank top or an undershirt on Merle Haggard on his '*Big City*' record where he's sitting in a hotel room in New York City looking out the window—we don't get high marks for imagination. That cover always tested well for Merle. A

lot of times at shoots we play around with different wardrobes to see what you get.''

Did Ricky feel at ease with that look?

"I don't think he objected to it. All I know is six months later on the road he was selling those shirts for ten bucks.

"Ricky was always a very cooperative artist: gracious, always said 'thank you.' He was the type of guy you wanted to do things for. He was so appreciative. And they were here trying to eke out a living; and he was very dedicated. He would always say to me, if he said it to me once, he said it a thousand times: 'If you're waiting for me, then you're backing up.' That was always his line. It meant, 'Keep up with me.' ''

Blackburn emphasizes the importance of videos.

"We found, early on, the power of video. Ricky's was the first video I think I could hang my hat on and say, 'That sold records.' Looking back on it, I would never take the video out of the marketing plan. I mean it was a vital component.

"The other thing we did, which was marketing strategy, we decided, when we started to know he *can* sell some records, to do a tour in Texas, just took the state of Texas, and for six weeks he was not *allowed* to come out of the state of Texas. He was down there with a band, traveling in a station wagon pulling a trailer, and literally going from honky-tonk to dance hall around the state for a period of six weeks. Our feeling was that if we could get a base established for him down there—again, that George Strait market is so hot down there—then we could spread it, and meanwhile we can sell enough to kick off some revenue to finance page two. So for six weeks he's down there, in poverty conditions. He would call me about once a week and get homesick and wanna come home. I'd say, 'You can't come home yet.'

"Well, he thought it more of a sentence, you know, than a marketing strategy and, of course we'd have to explain to him what we were trying to do. It was easy for *me* to say, I wasn't living it. He and his wife are very close, and he was getting homesick to the point where I didn't think he'd make it through that six week period. I honestly didn't. We were takin' bets around the office to see what day he'd dump the tour but he stuck through it and it proved to be a good strategy, really built a base for him."

What is the one element that connects Ricky Van Shelton to his audience?

"Sincerity," is Blackburn's immediate response.

Of all the successful hunks, Ricky may be the one least understood by the veteran music industry people in Nashville.

"Music Row—our industry—what are we? Six blocks long? Three blocks wide?" Blackburn scowls. " . . . is not really in touch with the country music business from a fan standpoint at all. Give you an example: I can't tell you, in the last year, meetings take place [in which people say]: 'If we could get Bonnie Raitt to cross over and get country radio to play it, then we could be hip.' Well, one, country radio's not gonna do that, and two, why should we? I mean we're hip without [that]."

On Music Row Rick also hears statements like, "One thing we don't need is another hat act." "We do research every month. Not here, but out there:

Wichita, Caspar, Wyoming, Peoria, places like that. The industry doesn't have a clue that the public out there is saying, 'Give me all you got.' So I went out and signed one named Tracy Lawrence. And then The Row said, 'Another hat act! My gosh!' All I know is, we're gold in eight months time. So you can't look on Music Row as having a pulse on much of anything. I'm serious about that.

"So, by them not understanding a phenomenon like Ricky Shelton, I understand that. Then again, you find you can't make decisions from a luncheon table at Maude's Courtyard [a fashionable restaurant a block or two off Music Row that recently closed its doors]. You're in a vacuum there. So when's the last time you saw me at Maude's Courtyard? I don't do it. Nothin' against the restaurant, you understand.''

Blackburn learns a lot about "out there" from his artists.

"When you take an artist that's out and about, that's doing 150–200 dates a year, it could be Ricky Van Shelton or Tracy Lawrence, you gotta listen to them some, because they're face to face with that buying public a helluva lot more than you are . . . So, I talk to them about that a lot. Let's take the temperature out there. They are sort of an eyes and ears thing.

"Music Row as an industry down here is pretty insulated when it comes to the fan base. You can probably ask a hundred people around here, 'What's a line dance?' They have no idea what a line dance is. Five miles away at the Wrangler—country music night club—you'll see the country consumer out there doing a line dance every night of the week. That's how they use country music. It's a dance. Go and see it. Dancing is a big usage factor now in country music.''

Rick Blackburn is one of country music's more knowledgeable record executives. He's also a great admirer of Ricky Van Shelton. It's no surprise to Blackburn that over the past five years Ricky has been among the most consistently successful record sellers in country music. Early in his career the marketing strategists Blackburn says so much about helped give Ricky the kind of publicity blitz that he needed. In more recent years his albums have, very quietly, one after another, gone platinum.

But Ricky Van Shelton has yet to show us all he's got. As this is being written, Van Shelton has a new single out. It's ''Wear My Ring Around Your Neck,'' a remake of one of Elvis's records. It may not be art, but it shows a rockin' side of Ricky Van Shelton that radio listeners haven't heard much. The fans who buy his records know the rockin' side of Ricky, and I suspect we'll all be hearing more of the same if this one clicks. There will be other pleasant surprises from Ricky over the next few years. I do not believe this hunk has peaked.

11

Vince Gill

WHO ARE THE HOTTEST OF THE HOT COUNTRY hunks? Well, of course, it depends upon what month of what year you happen to choose them. I've chosen to devote separate chapters to nine of them, either because they are extremely hot at the time this book is being written, or because they have been such an important force in the powerful surge of country music today.

All nine of these artists are marvelous solo vocalists. Eight of them have pursued careers focused on their skills as solo performers and songwriters. The ninth spent years as a session and road musician and backup singer. Eight of them have strong roots in the honky-tonk tradition of country music. The ninth one is steeped in love of bluegrass.

This bird of a different feather is Vince Gill. In recent years, Vince has made the big jump from being an airplay artist to being a selling artist. This is an unusual transition. Most of the time, when an artist gets top ten country radio hits, either the folks like him enough to start buying his albums then, or they never do, no matter how many number one singles the artist has.

Vince was born in 1957 in Norman, Oklahoma, not far from where Garth Brooks was raised. His father was a lawyer and banjo picker and Vince grew up playing bluegrass. His life may be music but his passion is golf. In his younger years he dreamed of being a professional golfer, and probably still dreams of it. Instead of committing himself in that direction, graduation from high school found him off to Louisville, Kentucky, to play with a group called the Bluegrass Alliance. A year later he headed for Los Angeles, where he eventually became a member of the pop/country group Pure Prairie League. In the course of his long stay on the West Coast he gained an awesome reputation as a studio musician and backup singer. He also became friends with a number of country talents whose friendship would continue long after they had all made the move from southern California to Middle Tennessee.

One of these talents is a fellow named Carl Jackson, who spent a number of years on the road picking with Glen Campbell. Like Vince, Mississippi-reared Carl Jackson has bluegrass roots. At the age of fourteen he was playing with the great bluegrass duo Jim and Jesse and to this day much of his music bears that influence. Carl has in recent years become one of Nashville's most prosperous songwriters, with songs recorded by many of the country biggies. And his friendship with Vince Gill goes well back to their L.A. days.

''I went to work with Glen in 1972 and of course Vince was out there doin' his thing and we ran into

Vince Gill

each other a couple of times, really didn't become close or anything, and Vince signed his deal with RCA there in, I guess, what, the early eighties?

"I didn't really know Vince that well until that first little mini-LP he did on RCA, which I sang harmony on. Emory Gordy produced it and Emory was a friend and he called and asked me if I would sing harmony on it and, I had heard about Vince and was more than happy to do it, and then, after hearing those sides that Emory had done, I mean, he [Vince] just blew me away—his vocal ability *and* his playing ability."

At the time Carl Jackson was living in California there was a very strong and talented country contingent there that included folks like Vince, Emmylou Harris, Rodney Crowell, Rosanne Cash, and others. Many of them have since moved from California to Nashville, including a number of producers and record executives like Emory Gordy, Jimmy Bowen, Jim Ed Norman, Bruce Hinton, and James Stroud. The influence of all these people on the Nashville music scene has been incalculable.

They have a different set of experiences to draw upon than those who have spent their entire careers doing music business the Nashville way. Bowen, for example, has had a great deal to do with increasing the dollar commitment of New York and L.A. record companies to their Nashville divisions. During the decade he has been in Nashville, he has headed the country divisions of four major labels, and each one is very different from what it had been earlier.

Although the performers who have moved from California to Nashville generally have been happy with their new life-style, and fit in pretty well with the Nashville-bred artists, many of them have understandably maintained their ties with those they knew in their West Coast days.

"We did an album together with Emmylou Harris, *The Angel Band*, myself and Vince and Emory Gordy. That was a great project and great fun. We just gathered at Emmy's place and sat around in a circle and sang gospel songs. I don't know if we really thought at the time that it would come out. It was just kind of for our own pleasure... It got real good and was later released on Warner Brothers."

Do Vince and Carl get together much to write? Carl's answer provides an insight into the sensitivities and protocol involved in cowriting songs in Nashville, Tennessee.

"Recently we finally got together after all these years and wrote a song for his new project. It's called 'No Future In The Past.' We had a great time doin' it. You know, I never *would* call Vince and say 'Let's write.' I didn't want him to think, 'well, now I'm a big artist so Carl calls and says let's get together.' And he was the same way because I've had a lot of success writin' here lately and he kinda felt that way [about writing with me now that I'm hot]."

Vince Gill was "discovered" by his fellow artists and songwriters long before country fans began to hear his music on the radio.

"I always knew," Carl smiles, "from the first time I heard Vince, that it would be no problem to have hits with Vince Gill. I felt that a lot of times—and I don't mean to point fingers at anybody—that he was kind of misdirected and, maybe it came from Vince. Because he is so talented. The guy can do anything. He can do any form of music. He can *play* any form of music. But he was signed as a *country* artist.

"I can tell you a little story that happened. About two or three years ago when the *When I Call Your Name* album was out. I hadn't heard the album at the time. I had only heard the single that was out, a thing he wrote with Rosanne [Cash]. Nice tune but kinda pop. It was out there and kinda doin' okay but not selling any records, you know, but [being played] quite a bit. Anyway he sends me over a copy of the album, cause we're gonna get together and rehearse for a show. Of course, 'When I Call Your Name' was on the album. I hear the song and I'm like [thinking] man, this is incredible. This is great! So we go to rehearsal and we start rehearsing the song. I'm lucky enough to get to do Patty's [Loveless] parts. I told him, 'Vince, you're in the country music business. You're signed as a country artist, whether you like it or not. Why do you not release this song? This is an absolute smash.'

"He said, 'Do you really think so?' Those were his exact words and I said, 'Vince, this is it!' And he said, 'Well, they're talkin' about this bein' the next single.' It hadn't been firmed up and decided at the time. Sure enough, they came with it and the rest is history.''

It might surprise fans when a song like ''When I Call Your Name'' becomes a career-making hit for an artist, that neither the artist nor the record people involved with him realized that they had *the* song just sitting on that album waiting to be pulled as a single so it could skyrocket to the top. But in fact, the people in the business often get so close to the songs on the album that they lose the ability to listen to them the way a fan would.

''I think there isn't a better singer out there. He's wonderful, but it doesn't excite *me* to hear Vince sing pop music. I mean, it's good, but the [country] songs he's doin' now, nobody could ever do them better. That's my opinion of why he's so big now, why he finally broke [as a selling artist after years of being more an airplay artist].''

In the fifties, sixties, and seventies a number of country artists, notably the aforementioned Eddy Arnold and Ray Price, but also Dolly Parton and others, attempted to widen their audiences by singing more pop-flavored tunes. These attempts were resented by

hard country fans who felt that they were being abandoned, that the artists they'd loved for so long
had gotten "above their raisin'." These fans also
viewed skeptically pop artists who, having run their
course as pop recording artists, were now attempting
to keep their recording careers alive by going
country.

Country fans view their artists differently today.
Even dedicated country acts like George Strait grew
up listening to and performing different kinds of music. As Carl Jackson pointed out, Vince Gill can do

many kinds of music. But his country music background is so strong and obvious that he requires no purity test to decide whether he is qualified to be a country star.

Jackson believes that when Vince Gill started giving the fans country records instead of pop sounding records, his career took off. "You don't try to force feed 'em down another market," he says. "I really believe that with all my heart. It has nothing to do with it being good. It has to do with my daddy cares nothing about pop music."

You can get number one country records with pop songs, he believes, but the country fans don't go out and *buy* those records. "I think radio dictates too much of what comes out as singles. [They'll take a record] to number one and it sells nothing. But if you get behind a 'When I Call Your Name', a 'Pocket Full Of Gold' [two major Vince Gill releases], if you get behind those records in a country market, not only can they [take it to the top of the charts but] it'll produce with the people. Those kinds of [country] songs are tied directly to the heartstrings—they're tied directly to the wallet. I mean, they'll whip into Tower [record stores] and get that, whereas the pseudocountry, they don't."

Vince Gill was successful as a studio picker long before he achieved success as a solo recording artist. Having pursued a solo career as long as he did, was there a sense of change in his life when his recording career finally began to go right for him?

"Vince, to me, has never changed from the first time I ever met him till now . . . We talked about it a little bit. You know, congratulations on your—you

know—happy for you—but when Vince and I get together we'd rather talk about golf or baseball. I've
said things like, 'Nobody deserves it more, and I'm
so happy for you.' ''

Given Vince Gill's wide musical vocabulary, it's
easy to wonder just how dedicated to country music
he is. Carl Jackson has no doubts about the musical
heart of Vince Gill.

''We were in Florida doing 'Church Street Station'.
We walked over to a golf shop to get some new clubs
or whatever and we got on the subject of music; we
were talking about different singers and he used the
term, 'That guy has been to bluegrass school.' Emmy
uses that expression, you know it's like, Vince's vocal
abilities come from that background. He loves Flatt
and Scruggs, the Stanley Brothers, and that type of
stuff and that's where Vince's roots for music come
from.''

And what is that bluegrass school that makes Vince
so different from the honky-tonk type singers we've
been talking about throughout this book?

''One particular thing, and this is a small thing, is
that in mixing harmonies on a record, a lot of the
records that you turn on, the harmonies are kinda
there as, literally, a background. It's like, is there harmony on there or not? The bluegrass thinking is more
the 'When I Call Your Name' mix where, when the
harmony comes in, harmony really becomes harmony
rather than a background.''

He means that on bluegrass harmonies the singing
parts are so nearly equal in volume level that it sounds
like a three-part blend rather than a solo voice backed
up by two or three supporting voices. ''That's one

thing. All the little trills and things that Vince does, and I do, and Marty Raybon [of Shenandoah] does, and Joe Diffie does, all these guys come out of bluegrass. All these things come from those old bluegrass standards and mountain tunes. A lot of people tend to think that if you sing high, that's bluegrass. Well, no. Vince comes out of a bluegrass background and his voice is very bluegrass sounding but it's not because it's high.

"And [in spite of the bluegrassy harmonies] his records are certainly not bluegrass. They're country."

Where does bluegrass end and country begin?

"I'm a real black and white guy. To me a bluegrass band is totally acoustic, first of all. It's banjo, fiddle, mandolin, acoustic guitar, and upright bass; occasional dobro or whatever, and that is bluegrass one hundred percent. With tight harmonies—so if you want to base it like a lot of people think, you can take a record like 'When I Call Your Name' and because the vocals and the harmonies are one hundred percent bluegrass, do we say the record is one hundred percent bluegrass? No, we don't. Because, bluegrass don't have steel [guitar]. Sorry, they just don't. So, in my mind anyway, I can say where bluegrass ends and country starts. You know everybody has a different opinion on that."

What is it about Vince Gill that's different from the other hunks?

"First of all, he's one of the best guitar players in the world. Now Vince plays good mandolin. He's not a great mandolin player. He plays a little dobro. None of those [other hot country hunks] are great musicians. And Vince is a musician's musician. He's *that* good."

And unlike many of the other hunks, Vince has not made becoming a star the grand focal point of his career.

"He's always had a kind of 'whatever happens happens,' attitude. If it happens it happens, and if it don't it don't, and I'm havin' a good time, and I'm gonna play my golf—I like that. I think that's just another facet of Vince that makes him Vince. I know that when we were in here [Carl's writing office at Famous Music on Nashville's 16th Avenue South] writin' he was talkin' about how he's gone so much and he's not gettin' to do a lot of the real fun things that he needed to do for awhile but of course the success level has [forced him to be out on the road that much more]. He's workin' hard but I still think that Vince would rather be on the golf course than anywhere else. He's a carefree guy who loves to have a good time. A great sense of humor."

If most of the hunks have their roots in the Lefty Frizzell-Merle Haggard tradition, and Ricky Van Shelton to some degree fills the Jim Reeves niche in country music, is there a tradition that Vince Gill relates to?

"I haven't talked to Vince at all about this, but I would have to think—and this is gonna be out of the bluegrass field now, however they did a lot of records that charted country—I would have to think that Vince has spent an awful lot of time listening to Bobby Osborne." For those of you who are recent converts to country music, Bobby Osborne sings high tenor for the Osborne Brothers, a bluegrass duo that have been regulars on the Grand Ole Opry for many years and may be best known for having had the first

chart record of the Boudleaux and Felice Bryant anthem, ''Rocky Top.''

''In Bobby's time, man, he *was* the best, oh man, what a singer. The other night we did the Country Music Foundation special for the Hall of Fame, and Vince wasn't able to be there, but I was there with Emmy, and they had a tape of Vince and he sang 'Makin' Plans,' the Johnny Russell tune and, believe me, he had listened to the Osbornes' record. He sang it so great. That [Bobby Osborne] might be an odd selection because you really consider them bluegrass but they certainly did a lot of top ten records in the country field.''

Jackson feels a strong bond for Vince Gill the person that goes beyond the talents of Vince Gill the musician.

''If I had to make a list [of Vince's qualities] I'd probably put 'nice guy' at the top of the list. I think that if I needed him for something, I think if there was any way in the world he would do it. I have a song on Garth's album *Ropin' The Wind*, a song called 'Against The Grain.' Vince played on the demo for me. We were sittin' around talkin' and I had this [demo] session comin' up and I can't remember if I jokingly said, 'Hey man, you wanna play guitar on it,' or if he brought it up. I mean, he was already hot! [already a star] But he said, 'Man I'd love to,' he came over and played, wouldn't take any money, he just wanted to. He probably helped to get 'Against The Grain' cut.

''Ah—sense of humor. When I think of Vince, I laugh. You know when he walks in, there's somethin' goin' on from the time he's here. He's constantly joking. And laughing. Imitatin' Elvis . . . ''

Does that translate into his stage act?

''Out of the time I've been around him, that seems to be the time when Vince is his most serious. On the stage. Little things can bother Vince a lot on stage. He strives for perfection. And I admire that in him because I'm the same way.''

Like so many of the top country hunks, Vince Gill is a member of the Grand Ole Opry. Nowadays there's no monetary advantage in being a member of the Opry, especially if you're already a star. One has to believe that Vince, like the others, loves the Opry and the tradition that goes with it.

He's married to the former Janis Oliver of the group Sweethearts of the Rodeo, and the story of their courtship is heart-warming (as told by Cynthia Sanz and Jane Sanderson in *People* magazine).

''One night in 1977, in a Redondo Beach, Calif., cafe, the Sweethearts were opening for Vince's band, and Vince and Janis passed each other on the stairway to the stage. 'I caught her eye, and she caught my eye, but I don't think she liked my eyes as much as I liked hers.' Vince says. 'I was pretty smitten with her and asked her out for almost three years, but she never would go out with me. I guess I was a pretty big hillbilly to her.' ''

'' 'It just wasn't right then,' says Janis, who already had a boyfriend and regarded Vince, then 19 to her 22, as a tad too young. But the pair became friends, she says, and 'when the guy I was seeing and the girl he was seeing dumped us at the same time, we decided it might be a good time to give it a whirl. It didn't take two weeks for us to see that it was serious.' "

They were married in 1980. In 1983 they moved to Nashville, two music professionals on parallel but unconcomitant courses. The Sweethearts got radio hot while Vince developed a fairly small group of admirers as a solo artist and ubiquitous backup singer. When an artist's career is happening, he or, in this case, she gets a lot of phone calls, a lot of attention, a lot of admiration. It's hard for the other partner if she or, in this case, he is not shining at the time.

Rick Blackburn, former head of CBS records in Nashville, signed the Sweethearts of the Rodeo to their record deal, and so he spent some time with Vince, watching him cope.

"Their first album had some success. They were touring and Vince at that point—poor Vincie—was sort of like Mr. Mom. He was in between labels—I believe he was on RCA fixing to go to MCA. Nothing was really happening [for Vince] and so he became kind of a Mr. Mom and Janis was out touring and the group, Sweethearts of the Rodeo, was starting to do something. I remember having some conversations with Janis and it was an adjustment for both of them. In particular with Vince, partly because she was gone a lot and partly because Vince had tried desperately to get his career off the ground and, here comes Janis barely trying and she's taking off.

"So I called Vince on the phone and asked him to come down to the office. And he did. He comes lumbering in at about 9:30 in the morning and sat there, had a little coffee and talked, and I tried to explain to him, I said, 'I really appreciate your support with Janis because she's out there trying to support the project [record business-speak for 'help make the group a hit'] and I know it's tough on you. I want you to know that anything I can do to help you through this process, let me know.' Vince never complained about it, [he just said] 'Well, I hope it works.' Then we talked about his career some. I think he was going into the studio with Tony Brown. Tony Brown is a great record producer. And I said, 'You know, you're with the right guy, you really are. It's just a matter of your time and your turn. It's gonna come and you and Tony'll figure it out. Once you identify your sound, what the Vince Gill sound is ... I mean, look at you, you're a good-looking guy, the women are gonna go for it; your turn is coming.'

"He was [saying], 'Well, I sure hope so, but I don't know if it's going to or not. But I sure hope it does 'cause I'm gonna keep trying, keep in there, if I can ever get Janis home long enough to where I can make a record.' I'll never forget that conversation I had with Vince. It hasn't been that many years ago; and sure enough...I ran into Janis the other day, and now it's, 'Vince has gotta rehearse again!'"

Now it's Vince getting all the publicity and attention while we're not hearing much from the Sweethearts of the Rodeo. "It just tells you how cyclical the business is," Blackburn continues. "But Vince had tremendous patience. He was very supportive of Janis. And that was a very tough time [for him]. And now, I know, she's very supportive of him." No doubt Vince, Janis, and their young daughter Jennifer will move through this phase as they've moved through years of previous phases.

How big can Vince Gill get? His songwriting, his musicianship, his musical awareness, and his terrific vocal skills mean that he will sound good no matter what he does. One guarantee is that he will not fall into a rut. Each album will be different from the last. It will be interesting to hear what his albums are sounding like five years from now.

12

Billy Ray Cyrus

IN 1955 A YOUNG KID BY THE NAME OF ELVIS PRESLEY was making a pretty big name for himself around the South. People didn't quite know what he was. In fact, he was often billed as ''The Hillbilly Cat,'' which meant that he was a little bit country and a little bit rock 'n roll.

Generally, the kids liked him but quite a few adults did not. His first appearances on the Louisiana Hayride were not well received and later, when he made his one appearance on the Grand Ole Opry, the diehards there certainly were not enchanted. In early 1956 he exploded into the national consciousness and he remains there to this day. His early record sales were great but not unique. People forget that during Elvis's early hit period a young man named Johnny Mathis was also a mighty power on the pop charts.

Elvis was more than just a rock star, he was the living symbol of the rock 'n roll revolution, so it was Elvis who absorbed much of the praise *and* condemnation until, at last, adult America accepted rock 'n roll as a legitimate part of the popular music scene.

Although Elvis's popularity diminished during the

hippie era, his legendary status was safe. Few people were surprised by the stunning adulation lavished on the King following his death. There will never be another Elvis, said his fans, only Elvis imitators.

And then, in the spring of 1992, Billy Ray Cyrus made a debut like no other artist before him. But he was not a complete surprise to everybody.

On the second of April in 1992, just before the Billy Ray explosion, I walked into the offices of *Music Row* magazine, and there I heard the voice of a prophet. I felt that David Ross, publisher of the magazine and a thoughtful observer of the country music scene, would get my research into this book off to a flying start, so I turned on the tape recorder and listened.

"I don't know if this is gonna fit what you wanted to hear or not," he said, "but I think what's really interesting right now is that there are so many uh, 'hunks' on the periphery that are just fixing to break through as we speak. . . . I wonder if it's as important to know who they are, at this stage, as the fact that there are so many of them out there that seem to be knocking on the door; . . . it's kinda like the middle sixties, early seventies when guitar players were so in vogue; all of a sudden every kid on the corner had a guitar and was trying to play Jimi Hendrix licks somehow. Now everybody's trying to get out there and be a country hunk."

He paused and thought for a moment. "There's a new kid over at Mercury as well, Billy Ray Cyrus . . ."

"I think I saw a picture of him," I interrupted. He ignored me.

" . . . has this new song called 'Achy Breaky Heart.' I think he could be huge."

And then he went on to other things. How could I have known that for a short moment he had opened the curtain and shown me the future of country music? I remembered a day back in 1955, as a child one winter in Florida when I was visiting a friend and heard "Mystery Train" on the radio.

"Who is that?" I asked him.

"Elvis Presley," he responded. The strange name bounced off my cranium like a rock and left me stunned, imaging a black man, perhaps a guy who looked a little like a smaller, wiry version of Bo Diddley.

"I think he could be huge," said David Ross on that cool, early spring day. According to my information, "Achy Breaky Heart" shipped on April 6, went gold in the middle of May, and hit the pop charts May 25, the first country single to go pop since Willie and Julio back in 1984.

The album, *Some Gave All*, shipped platinum toward the end of May, hit the top of the pop charts a couple of weeks later and by August 12 had been the number one album in America for ten consecutive weeks. Sales were nearing four million, America's young females were going out of their minds, and the signs indicated that the whole thing was about to start all over again in Europe.

Never in the history of recorded music had a debut album sold as fast or furiously as *Some Gave All*. As this book is being written, Billy Ray's music is making so much noise in Europe that his people are scheduling a European tour for him. The word is that Garth,

Billy Ray Cyrus

who has not yet penetrated the musical consciousness of Europe, will follow suit. It's very likely that the new hunk will finally prepare Europe to accept Garth and the rest of the hunks, something that part of the world has been avoiding up to now.

It's difficult for fans to understand that a brand new superstar is simply a person who just a short time ago lived his life a bit like you and I do. We might gain a little perspective by going back to December 30, 1990, shortly after he received "the best Christmas gift in the Tri-State this year—an eight-album, live tour contract with Mercury-Polygram Records."

The occasion was a Billy Ray interview with Cathie Shaffer, "Today's Living" Editor of the *Ashland* (Kentucky) *Independent*. Keep in mind that Billy Ray was still more than fifteen months away from the explosion that changed his life forever.

The headline of the piece was, "Flatwoods man gets record contract." The subhead was "April Ashland show still on tap," as if a brand new recording contract meant such instant riches that he would immediately suspend all local concert commitments.

"I'm ready to go to work," he told Shaffer in a telephone interview. "It's taken me ten good years to get to this point, ten years of concentrating on this as my goal and going at it."

Remember, all he's done to this point in the recording business is make a deal with a major record company. Dozens of country artists do that each year, and then nobody ever hears of them again.

" 'This is my break to the big time, but it's just the beginning,' he says. 'We'll be announcing the contract this week, but that's like a ground breaking. We've still got a heck of a building to build.

'This is when the work starts. Let me get some gold and platinum albums under my belt and then I'll celebrate.' "

Billy Ray was right about the ground breaking part. Several months passed before the *Some Gave All* album was recorded, and then ten more months before it was finally released. During that time, as one might imagine, Billy Ray got antsy. His manager, Jack McFadden, told it this way to Michael McCall for the *Los Angeles Times*.

"Billy Ray kept saying, 'Let me out of the chute, let me get out there and sing.' He believed in his music. Here I had an artist who believed he could sell product, but he didn't have any product out. He had finished it, he was proud of it, but nobody was allowed to hear it."

Remember, he's been knocking on the door for ten years and somebody has finally let him in. He's past thirty and feeling it's about time something in his life went right.

"That's the time period when, if I didn't actually lose my mind, I did the closest thing," Cyrus recalled in the *Times* article. "My wife decided she wanted a divorce. I had an album in the can. It was just sitting on the shelf, and I didn't know when or if it would come out. . . . All I could do was keep playing the clubs [around Ashland]."

Cyrus even tried driving down to Nashville and nagging them into putting the album out. But the folks at Mercury Records were trying to figure out how to break him out of the pack. Mercury has always been regarded as the junior partner of all the major record labels with Nashville offices. Over the years they had never managed to achieve the power or respect in country music of say, CBS, RCA, MCA or Warner Brothers. They knew that his first release would have to compete with the records of the other hot country hunks. Yes, yes, you put out a great single, and yes, you create a great video, but everybody else thinks they're putting out great singles and videos. What's gonna make Billy Ray seem different?

At this point, Claudia Mize took a giant step into the history of country music. Claudia has been in the Nashville music business for a number of years. She is competent and well-liked. Record company administrators get neither the glamour nor the glory. But

Claudia should get a monument. One day, while Mercury staffers were discussing how to do *something* to make Billy Ray stand out to radio and video programmers, it was Claudia who suggested a dance contest.

If Claudia deserves a monument, marketing director Steve Miller deserves at least a medal for knowing a good idea when he hears one. In the eyes of many industry pros, country music and dance promotions hadn't been copacetic since the heyday of western swing. But over the past few years, the Texas-Oklahoma dance tunes of George Strait, Clint Black, and others had brought the two-step back to the country music clubs around America.

And so the label hired choreographer Melanie Greenwood to create a line dance to the beat of "Achy Breaky Heart." And why not? Somebody created the waltz. The tango. The lambada.

"On February 14 . . ." according to McCall, "twenty-six leading dance spots across the United States began playing a tape of Cyrus' performance along with an instructional tape showing how to do the so-called Achy Breaky Line Dance." Three weeks later Mercury got the video premiered on The Nashville Network and Country Music Television, two premier country video outlets.

" 'Everybody went crazy over it,' Miller contends. 'No record company had gone to the country nightclubs at that point with anything on this kind of scale . . . The clubs and their clients responded by embracing the dance and along with it, the song and the artist.' "

Having primed the pump, on April 6 Mercury re-

leased the single and Billy Ray poured down on America like Niagara.

Billy Ray was a bit dubious about launching his recording career on the steps of a dance. And others who had *their* doubts weren't necessarily very nice in expressing them. Someone suggested in the *New York Times* that "If Garth Brooks is the new Elvis of country music, then Billy Ray Cyrus is the new Fabian." A *Rolling Stone* writer complained to Robert Oermann that "Achy Breaky Heart" sounded like a demo and Travis Tritt kvetched that the song "does not make much of a statement." Travis went further: "What we're going to have to do to be popular in country music is get into an ass-wiggling contest..."

Travis should have known better. He will sell *more* records with Billy Ray on the scene, not fewer, and

as Billy Ray breaks down the gates in Europe, Travis
Tritt should be able to walk right into a bonanza.

We've talked about how hot Billy Ray is and how
he got hot, but who is he and how did he get
"discovered?"

He's from Flatwoods, a town of a little less than
eight thousand people in northeastern Kentucky, just
across the river from Ironton, Ohio, and not far from
Huntington, West Virginia.

He is the son of Kentucky state assemblyman Ron
Cyrus, who was divorced from Billy Ray's mother,
Ruth Ann, when Billy Ray was six. Apparently Billy
Ray's two great ambitions were to be a major league
catcher like Johnny Bench or to be a singing star. The
press makes a big deal out of that ("if singing hadn't
grabbed Billy Ray's achy breaky heart he might today
be breaking pitchers' hearts with his bat" might be a
typical newspaper hook) but if you think about it, millions of boys across the face of America have
dreamed those dreams through most of this century.

He attended Georgetown State College in Kentucky
but dropped out at the age of twenty and bought a
guitar. Without a background in professional entertaining some probably thought he was going crazy.
But what he was doing was making a commitment
instead of drifting. That's what college means for
many kids. It takes a certain amount of courage to
make that kind of commitment because anyone who
does is going to hear an awful lot of "YOU QUIT
WHAT IN ORDER TO BE A WHAT?!"

He started playing local clubs and in 1984 moved
to Los Angeles. There he sold cars and watched other
people make it. In 1986 he returned to eastern Ken-

tucky, formed a band, and found a steady gig at a club in Huntington. His music was partly his own songs, partly Bob Seger, and partly Lynyrd Skynyrd. I have mentioned before the sound instincts and common sense that so many hot country hunks have brought to their careers. Billy Ray, who was already able to conquer an audience, probably understood the need to build a base of loyal followers. He had decided to seek a recording career in Nashville, three-hundred miles away, and wore out a lot of rubber commuting to Music City on his days off.

The idea is to meet someone who knows someone who knows someone who can help. Billy Ray met the daughter of Del Reeves, a veteran Opry star. Del introduced Cyrus to talent manager Jack McFadden, who has been working with Buck Owens for decades. McFadden signed Billy Ray and toward the end of 1989 started pitching tapes by Billy Ray to the major labels, *all* the major labels, some of them several times.

Rejection of tape auditions is no major setback to an old hand like McFadden. He knew that they were going crazy over Billy Ray up in the Tri-state area so he started persuading Nashville record men to take in the spectacle. At least one very good A & R man passed on Billy Ray live in person. Then Buddy Cannon, a Mercury executive, made the pilgrimage and returned a convert.

Buddy's boss, Harold Shedd, went up to check on the excitement. One story has it that the crowd was so wild Harold thought they might be faking it for his benefit so he made another trip up before he decided to sign Billy Ray.

Joe Scaife and Jim Cotton were chosen to produce the album. "Achy Breaky Heart" was one of the cuts. Don Von Tress, who wrote the song, had been sending songs to Nashville without success for over a decade, which may say more about the futility of pitching songs from out of town than it does about Don Von Tress's songwriting talents. And in case you're wondering, the answer is yes, "Achy Breaky Heart" could take care of Don Von Tress for the rest of his life, even if he never has another hit. But he will have other hits, depend on it.

A measure of Billy Ray's success is all the stories and rumors about him that have sprouted like weeds after a July rainstorm. Most of them will die away, to be replaced by a new crop the next rain—or at least, the next album.

Is he the next Elvis? Of course not. Elvis was a man, not a music category. Billy Ray Cyrus is a unique entry in the country music sweepstakes. He is already, as David Ross prophesied, "huge." Nobody, anytime, anywhere, has sold four million records earlier in his or her recording career than Billy Ray Cyrus. And this is just the first chapter. I can't wait to read the book.

13

In Closing

MONTH AFTER MONTH AFTER MONTH GARTH Brooks dominated the pop and country album charts. Every so often, a pop album might knock Garth's *Ropin' The Wind* out of the top spot, only to see it return to the top the following week.

But on the country charts, there were no challengers. *Ropin' The Wind, No Fences*, and *Garth Brooks* stayed numbers one, two, and three until, one shocking week in the spring of 1992, a brand new album smashed through to knock him out of the top spot for the first time in more than half a year. And who was the hunk who did it?' Tweren't no hunk at all but rather a hunkette named Wynonna Judd.

After a few weeks at the top she gave back the top spot to Garth. But she had made her point, and country music's point, because she was also top ten on the *Billboard* 200 that tracks the top albums regardless of genre. Country was still exciting, fresh and hot because its artists were. And Wynonna was additional proof (as if any were needed) that the girls of country music offer a solid challenge to the boys. The same week Garth moved back on top,

George Strait's brand new album *Holding My Own* broke into the country album chart at the number five slot, and the top 200 chart at forty-three. Among the hottest country singles that week were Brooks & Dunn at number one, Little Texas, and Billy Ray Cyrus. To cap it all off, Billy Ray hit the *Billboard* pop charts that week as "Hot Shot Debut," the first country single to cross over to the pop charts in half a dozen years. Country was continuing to pump new blood into a business whose business *is* new blood.

And yet there were a couple of hand-sized clouds on this otherwise sunny horizon. I was having lunch with the head of artist development for the Nashville division of one of the major labels. He was excited because his label had just had hits on a pair of brand new acts, but he was just a little down.

"Country Music Television and TNN," he began, shaking his head, "just don't understand. Their formatting is really beginning to tighten up." He was worried that after years and years of playing the videos they like best, these terribly important outlets were becoming more concerned with playing it safe. People who play it safe spend a lot of time worrying that they may be the only ones playing a particular video or record, and that people tuning into their station will tune right out again. That kind of attitude makes a station more likely to play a mediocre video by an artist with a track record than a good video by a new artist. But when I took the opportunity to watch TNN or CMT, I felt that they were still showing the good stuff, regardless of whether the artist was new or established. My friend might merely have been annoyed because *his* label was having a problem getting a new artist played.

Also, a front page article in *Billboard* announced that, "After more than two years of unprecedented breakthroughs for new acts on country radio, country PDs [program directors] are finally making good on last year's warning that they would start breaking unfamiliar artists at a more moderate pace." The article went on to give figures showing that through most of 1991 country radio stations were wide open to brand new artists, but that by the spring of 1992 many key country stations were becoming much more cautious about playing new country artists.

Actually, that kind of thinking, if it prevails, is not a hand-sized cloud. More like a fire storm that could burn the heart right out of country if it really happens. Read this from the same article:

"Country PDs (program directors) say they're still song driven, not artist driven. They also say the challenge to breaking new artists is the release of *too much* good product, not too little." Wait a minute! Do you mean to tell us that there is so much great stuff on the radio that there is no room for more? We don't believe it. What you're really saying is that there is not enough room for great new records *and* new music from the familiar hunks. The lesson is, if the hottest hunk going puts out a stiff single, you have to lay off it and instead play the great new record by Mr. (or Ms.) First Time Artist. As long as there's another Alan Jackson, Travis Tritt, or Billy Ray Cyrus waiting in the wings with great music, then country music will have nothing to worry about *if* country radio and video continue to have the nerve to play the right stuff. But the moment programmers are afraid to go with something because it's new and fresh, then country music will be in trouble.

In the late eighties a bunch of brand new artists came in and sent a bunch of great old artists packing for Branson. Until that happened there were many singers out there getting top ten singles who couldn't sell two hundred thousand albums. Big record sales mean excitement—people so thrilled with an artist that they're willing to walk into a Tower or a Wal-Mart and plop down ten or fifteen dollars to hear the whole album. Number one records by artists who don't sell mean just the opposite—passive listeners who enjoy country music as elevator music, background music they half-listen to while they're on their way from home to the dentist's office.

Now I know that all this sounds like music business inside stuff. Fans are supposed to be like cows, contentedly munching on pasture grass that their betters have fenced off for them. But the reason country has gotten this big is that radio and video have set the fans loose on the open range, free to hear all these brand new artists over the air, and then pick and choose for themselves which ones they like. The result is a lot of new fresh sounds, and folks have shown their appreciation by going out and buying albums by the millions.

Country pundit Robert Oermann doesn't appear to be worried. "Can the country boom last or will it turn out to be just another 'Urban Cowboy' pop-culture fad?" he asks in his *Tennesseean* column.

"I think we've got something permanent this time," he insists. "So many stars in country music are selling well that it appears we've got a real shift in music fans' preferences.''

Well, we know that all good things come to an end, but like Robert Oermann, I believe the end of country's huge wave of popularity is nowhere in sight. The challenge is for the record labels to continue coming up with new music and new talent that is so good that radio and video cannot deny it. Oermann wrote about walking to his car after attending a concert on a college campus. On the way, he passed a fraternity house. ''The college boys,'' he said, ''were having a Friday-night party. You know what they had on the stereo? Clint Black.''

The artist who has the record people in Nashville positively daffy with anticipation is, of course, Billy Ray Cyrus.

What excitement! Walk into the A & R office of any major label in Nashville and you'll hear, ''We've got this new kid who is going to knock your socks off!'' They all believe they can find another act who can sell like Garth, or Billy Ray. And the sounds range from bluegrass to rockabilly and beyond. The Nashville music business has learned from its great mistake of the fifties. Never again will the country music industry attempt to bump a major artist off the country charts on the grounds of his being too pop, as it did in the days of Elvis and the rockabillies.

Once again country music has come up with entertainment magic. It makes us say to ourselves, wow, I wonder what the next one is gonna be like? And we're all absolutely confident that the next one is just over the horizon. What will he be like? Will he be another hat, like Garth or Clint or Alan? Will he be a rocker, like Travis Tritt or Billy Ray? Will he be a smoothie like Ricky Van? Or maybe another new direction, with a folk twist like James Taylor, or a group like the Byrds or the Eagles? Or maybe, the next hunk to break the bank out there will be a hunkette. There have never been as many solid selling female country artists as there are now.

Whoever it is, he (or she, or they) will have broad demographic appeal. Because what is especially exciting about country music today is that if you go to a Garth Brooks concert, you will find grayhairs sitting next to teenyboppers. College boys may well like Clint Black, but so do forty-five-year-old housewives. Is it possible that country in the nineties will be the first truly intergenerational middle-class pop music in forty years? Now there's an amazing thought, ain't it?

The Best in
Biographies
from Avon Books

IT'S ALWAYS SOMETHING
by Gilda Radner   71072-2/$5.95 US/$6.95 Can

**JACK NICHOLSON: THE UNAUTHORIZED
BIOGRAPHY** *by Barbara and Scott Siegel*
                                     76341-9/$4.50 US/$5.50 Can

STILL TALKING
by Joan Rivers   71992-4/$5.99 US/$6.99 Can

CARY GRANT: THE LONELY HEART
by Charles Higham and Roy Moseley
                                     71099-9/$5.99 US/$6.99 Can

I, TINA
by Tina Turner with Kurt Loder
                                     70097-2/$4.95 US/$5.95 Can

ONE MORE TIME
by Carol Burnett   70449-8/$4.95 US/$5.95 Can

PATTY HEARST: HER OWN STORY
by Patricia Campbell Hearst with Alvin Moscow
                                     70651-2/$4.50 US/$5.95 Can

SPIKE LEE
by Alex Patterson   76994-8/$4.99 US/$5.99 Can